DK GARDEN

TREES

RICHARD ROSENFELD

W9-ASK-558

DK

LONDON, NEW YORK,
MUNICH, MELBOURNE, DELHI

Series Editor Helen Fewster
Series Art Editor Alison Donovan
Project Editor Zia Allaway
Art Editor Ann Thompson
Designer Rachael Smith
Editor Jane Simmonds
Managing Editor Anna Kruger
Managing Art Editor Lee Griffiths
Consultant Louise Abbott
DTP Designer Louise Waller
Media Resources Lucy Claxton
Picture Research Samantha Nunn
Production Controller Mandy Inness
US Editor Christine Heilman
US Senior Editor Jill Hamilton
US Editorial Assistant John Searcy

First American Edition, 2004

Published in the United States by
DK Publishing, Inc.
375 Hudson Street
New York, New York 10014

04 05 06 07 08 10 9 8 7 6 5 4 3 2 1

A Cataloging-in-Publication record for this book
is available from the Library of Congress.

ISBN 0-7566-0357-9

Color reproduction by Colourscan, Singapore
Printed and bound in Italy by Printer Trento

Discover more at
www.dk.com

Gardening with trees

THERE IS A HUGE RANGE OF TREES, in all shapes and sizes, for gardens large and small, flamboyant and subdued. Evergreen or deciduous, trees are the best way of injecting height, shape and structure, summer shade, and long winter shadows across the lawn. And the most rewarding provide colored bark, flowers, fruits, flashy autumn leaves, and a tracery of winter stems.

Trees are a key part of garden design. They can offer a delightful change of pace by creating shady conditions for planting such flowers as bluebells and cyclamen, or for siting a garden seat. They can be used to denote an outer boundary, to signal the entrance to a completely different part of the garden, or to act as the focal point within a specific area, encapsulating its style and mood.

But probably the best reason for growing trees is that they inject year-round value and character. While perennials come and go, trees give a rich, textured sense of permanence in any garden situation.

A tree is a long-term investment. Before buying, check its final size, as well as its site and soil requirements, to ensure that it will become a first-rate feature.

◀ **Pealike flowers** hang in long clusters from *Laburnum* x *watereri* 'Vossii'.

◀ **Dazzling autumn colors** are a feature of many maples, including this spectacular *Acer tataricum* subsp. *ginnala*, which also has bright green summer foliage.

Spring

Several trees kick off the spring with a superb aerial mass of blossoms. The ornamental cherries offer a lively choice, especially *Prunus sargentii* (Sargent cherry), which gives a terrific show of pale pink flowers against red leaves. But if that's too tall for your garden, try *Amelanchier* x *grandiflora* 'Ballerina', with its beautiful clusters of white blossoms, or the weeping *Malus* x *scheideckeri* 'Red Jade', which gives an outburst of frothy white flowers.

Other stunning spring choices include the flowering magnolias, and there's now such a wide variety of choice specimens that it's worth checking specialist catalogs to see the full range. *Magnolia* 'Heaven Scent' has strongly scented flowers and *M. campbellii* has huge flowers up to 12in (30cm) wide. With the yellow flowers

An aerial mushroom of blossom lights up a Japanese yoshino cherry

of the laburnums, and the white blossoms of the Chinese *Davidia involucrata* (handkerchief tree), there's no excuse for missing a fun spring show in the treetops.

The highly prized, shapely *Cornus controversa* 'Variegata' has layered branches and colorful leaves.

Summer

Trees in summer add leafiness, shade, shape, and color. Most of the non-green kinds are in the purple-bronze range, such as the copper or purple beech (*Fagus sylvatica* 'Dawyck Purple' or *F. sylvatica* 'Riversii'), but you can be much bolder with *Populus* x *canadensis* 'Aurea' (Canadian poplar), which has bright golden yellow leaves, or a conifer with beautiful blue-tinged growth.

The forms of trees and the shade they cast vary, some providing a massive, chunky canopy, others contributing slim and stylish verticals that keep the eye moving. *Juniperus communis* 'Hibernica' is like a giant evergreen pencil, up to 15ft (5m) high and as wide as a dinner plate. For Oriental gardens there's the popular, pyramidal *Chamaecyparis obtusa* 'Nana Gracilis' (Hinoki cypress), and for formal gardens the tiered branches of *Cornus controversa* 'Variegata'. If you need trees that will let in more light, don't be afraid to have some pruning and sawing done to create a better shape.

Autumn and winter

The autumn show is one of the great sights of the gardening year, and you need at least one tree whose leaves do a quick color change, then fall, going out with a bang.

Sweetgums, Japanese maples, and tupelos all give an excellent show of foliage. As a bonus, the falling leaves of *Cercidiphyllum japonicum* (Katsura tree) emit a scent of caramel apples.

The startling white bark of *Betula utilis* var. *jacquemontii* reflects light into dull winter gardens.

The best winter trees have a tracery of branches or brightly colored bark. Bark colors range from the shiny copper brown of *Prunus serrula* (ornamental cherry) to the bright whites of the birches; plant them against a contrasting background. Other great winter trees include *Acer rufinerve*, with its green-and-white-striped branches, hollies for their blood-red berries and, above all, the evergreen *Eriobotrya japonica* (loquat) for its magnificent, leathery, tactile leaves, up to 12in (30cm) long.

The brilliant autumn show is one of the main reasons for planting *Crataegus persimilis* 'Prunifolia'.

Key considerations

TREES NEED TO RECEIVE the right amount of light, shelter, and rain, so you shouldn't plant them too close to walls or buildings, because such positions can be shady and dry (roots of poplar and willow can also damage foundations and pipes). Tender trees often need a warm wall, however, if they are to flourish in a cooler region. Finally, make sure a tree can be seen from several angles, especially when it is at its best.

Selecting trees

A tree will be a prime feature for many years, so take time to select the healthiest specimen, free of pests and diseases. Look for a good root system that's well spread out (not pointing in one direction), and balanced, strong, vigorous topgrowth on a straight, sturdy, undamaged stem. While it's tempting to buy the largest specimen available, a shorter, younger tree will be cheaper and will adapt more quickly to its new site. Trees are sold in three forms: bare-root, balled-and-burlapped, or in containers.

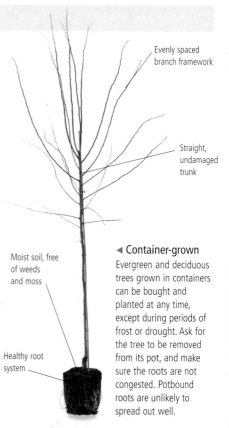

Evenly spaced branch framework

Straight, undamaged trunk

Moist soil, free of weeds and moss

Healthy root system

Bare-root ▼
Usually deciduous, bare-root trees have been lifted from open fields. Buy and plant them when dormant, from autumn to spring. Make sure the roots have not dried out.

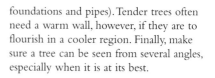

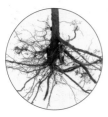

Balled-and-burlapped ▲
Deciduous trees over 12ft (4m) high and many evergreens are sold with protective wrapping over soil and roots. Make sure they are moist and plant from autumn to spring.

◄ Container-grown
Evergreen and deciduous trees grown in containers can be bought and planted at any time, except during periods of frost or drought. Ask for the tree to be removed from its pot, and make sure the roots are not congested. Potbound roots are unlikely to spread out well.

Digging the hole and planting

Before planting, select a site with free-draining soil and weed it well. When planting a container-grown tree, stand it in water for 30 minutes beforehand. Most trees benefit from staking to help them establish a good root system. Drive the stake in firmly before planting, positioning it on the side that receives the most wind. Remove it after two or three years. When planting in spring, add about 4oz (110g) of slow-release fertilizer to the soil.

1 Preparing the planting hole
Dig a circular hole 3–4 times the diameter of the root ball (2–3 times if balled-and-burlapped) and 1½ times its depth. Break up the soil around the sides and base.

2 Teasing out the roots
If planting container-grown tree, slide it gently out of its pot, lay it on the ground, and carefully tease out some of the outer roots to help the tree establish well.

3 Planting at the right depth
Insert the stake. Mix the removed soil with organic matter, adding some to the hole. Position the tree and make sure the top of the root ball is level with the soil.

4 Planting and finishing off
Gradually backfill around the tree with the rest of the soil and organic matter mixture, firming as you go. Attach the tree to the stake. Water well.

General care

YOUNG TREES NEED REGULAR CARE until they are established. Make sure they are watered regularly, and apply a thick mulch of shredded bark around the base in spring, covering an area 18in (45cm) larger than the root system and avoiding the trunk; this locks moisture in the soil, and suppresses weeds.

Young trees in poor soils need a slightly different approach. Feed them with an all-purpose fertilizer in early spring, being careful to follow the manufacturer's instructions. Then, after the next rain, spread a thick mulch of bark on the soil surface, avoiding the trunk. Keep the area weed-free.

Pruning young trees

Young deciduous trees are either sold ready-trained, with a clear stem and an array of branches high up, or in their earlier stage ("feathered"), when the branches are still on the stem. For feathered trees, you simply need to adopt a four-year pruning regimen (*see below*) to form a clear stem and an open arrangement of branches. Also prune to get rid of any dead, diseased, or damaged wood, and remove any vigorous shoots that are competing with the central stem.

Some feathered trees, such as beech, are best grown with their branches all the way up the stem. Only remove branches at the very base, and cut out crossing branches to give an open shape.

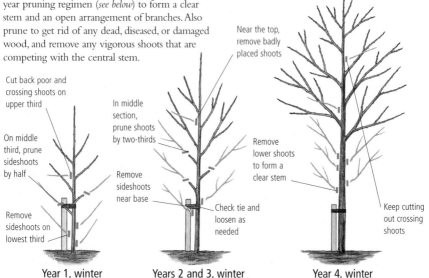

Cut back poor and crossing shoots on upper third

On middle third, prune sideshoots by half

Remove sideshoots on lowest third

In middle section, prune shoots by two-thirds

Remove sideshoots near base

Near the top, remove badly placed shoots

Remove lower shoots to form a clear stem

Check tie and loosen as needed

Keep cutting out crossing shoots

Year 1, winter

Years 2 and 3, winter

Year 4, winter

Thinning out old trees

At some point, established trees may need some pruning, either to correct lopsided growth or to remove suckers and any unhealthy or damaged branches. When growth is lopsided, prune the side with strong growth lightly at the branch tips, and prune back the side with poor growth hard, to stimulate lots of new, vigorous stems. Suckers are unwanted shoots growing from the roots or base; either scrape them off with your fingers or cut them back.

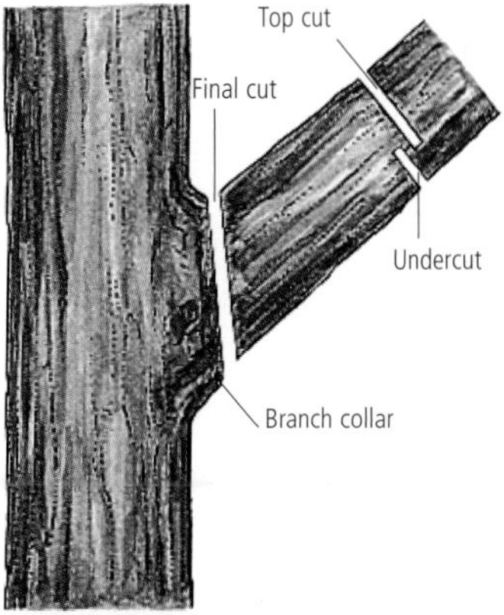

[Diagram with labels: Top cut, Final cut, Undercut, Branch collar]

Where to cut

Remove a branch more than 12in (30cm) in circumference in stages. This prevents the weight of the branch from causing it to fall, which may endanger you and others, and may tear the bark, damaging the tree. Do not cut into the branch collar; this contains the tree's natural defenses, which will help it to heal and protect it from any possible infection.

Precautions

• Carry out major work only on small trees; for larger ones, consult a professional arborist.
• Aim to work at ground level; take extra care if using ladders or climbing the tree.
• Avoid working in wet and slippery conditions.
• Keep children and pets away from the tree and from sawing equipment.

1 Making the undercut
With a pruning saw, first cut from under the branch, about 12in (30cm) from the trunk. Cut about a quarter of the way through.

2 Making the top cut
Cut through from above, about 1in (2.5cm) farther from the trunk than the first cut, to remove the heavy outer end of the branch.

3 Removing the stub
Make a small cut from below and then cut down from above until the cuts meet. Make this final cut clean and smooth, avoiding the collar.

Pollarding and coppicing

Some trees that have excellent colored bark or new stems, or attractive young leaves, can be pollarded or coppiced. These regular pruning techniques restrict the tree's size and force out new, vigorous growth. For a pollarded tree, cut off the established main trunk, usually at about head height, just before the emergence of the spring growth. This cut forces up a mass of thin shoots from the top. Remove this growth annually or every second year. Coppicing achieves the same effect, but the main pruning cut is made at ground level.

▲ **Pollarded tree**
Pollarded at about 4–5ft (1.2–1.5m), this willow (*Salix alba* 'Britzensis') has a superb array of new stems.

◀ **Hard pruning**
Cutting back to a low stem in spring encourages a compact, bushy habit. With trees such as this maple, the new stems will bear a mass of large, attractive leaves.

Multistemmed trees

Some trees with attractive bark (for example, the birches) are worth pruning so that they end up with several main stems instead of just one. In winter, cut back the main stem of a two-year-old tree, leaving a minimum of 3in (8cm) of growth above ground. The following winter, leave all but three of the best shoots, cutting off the rest at the base.

Bark on a multistemmed maple
The numerous trunks on this *Acer pensylvanicum* 'Erythrocladum' are striking, especially in winter.

Pests and diseases

While a well-maintained, healthy tree (given the conditions it requires) should have few if any problems, it is a good idea to know the symptoms of some of the major tree pests and diseases.

Prompt action can often stop problems from worsening. You can also take steps to improve growing conditions, which may help prevent pests and diseases from taking hold in the future.

Discolored leaves
Caused by drought, the shriveling and discoloring of leaves is particularly likely to affect young trees, or trees grown in containers. In some cases, leaves may drop. Water well, especially in dry spells.

Leaves with holes
Chewed-up leaves are usually caused by caterpillars. Either pick them off by hand or tackle by spraying. Several trees are likely to be attacked; they include maples, bays, and crabapples.

Malformed leaves
The new foliage on some trees is attacked by aphids. They are attracted by the sap but can be repelled by chemical sprays. Maples, bays, crabapples, and ornamental cherries are susceptible.

Peach leaf curl
An overwintering fungus causes the leaves of peach, nectarine, and almond trees to become puckered with red blisters in the spring and early summer. Sprays are available but have little impact.

Honey fungus
White, mushroom-scented fungus can appear at any time, just under the bark, with brown or black strands. Clumps of toadstools may appear around the tree. Remove the whole tree, including the roots.

Cracked stems or bark
When young or tender trees are exposed to icy temperatures, or to sudden temperature changes, the stems may split. Avoid this by planting tender trees in warm, well-protected sites.

A-Z of Trees

A

Abies koreana Korean fir

A GIANT SLENDER PYRAMID of an evergreen conifer, the Korean fir is grown for its shiny, dark green, needlelike leaves, which are silvery white underneath. The yellow male and reddish purple female flowers appear on the same tree in the spring, and are followed (from when the tree is about five years old) by cylindrical, upright cones, 2½in (6cm) long. The bark is dark gray-brown. Stately and imposing, the tree has a growth rate of approximately 24in (60cm) per year. Grow in a position sheltered from strong winds.

OTHER VARIETIES *A. koreana* 'Blauer Pfiff'; *A. koreana* 'Compact Dwarf'; *A. koreana* 'Flava'; *A. koreana* 'Nisbet'; *A. koreana* 'Oberon'; *A. koreana* 'Silberlocke'.

PLANT PROFILE

HEIGHT 30ft (10m)

SPREAD To 20ft (6m)

SITE Full sun

SOIL Moist but free-draining, slightly acidic

HARDINESS Z5–6 H6–5

Abies lasiocarpa var. *arizonica* 'Compacta' Corkbark fir

A

THIS SLOWER-GROWING, SMALLER VERSION of the evergreen conifer *A. lasiocarpa* var. *arizonica* makes a conical to oval shape, its branches densely covered with blue-gray needles. Because it puts on only about 1½in (4cm) per year, it is an excellent choice for a large rock garden. When it gets too big—and it might take ten years for it to reach 3½ft (1.1m) high—move it to another part of the yard. The flowers are followed by 3½in- (9cm-) long cones, but its key feature is the thick, corky bark. Grow in a sheltered position.

PLANT PROFILE
HEIGHT 10–15ft (3–5m)
SPREAD 6–10ft (2–3m)
SITE Full sun
SOIL Moist but free-draining, slightly acidic
HARDINESS Z5–6 H6–5

A · *Acacia dealbata* Mimosa, Silver wattle

In its native Australia the mimosa is a massive evergreen, up to 100ft (30m) high in ideal conditions, but in cooler climates it makes a much smaller tree or large shrub, growing to about 25ft (8m) high and 10ft (3m) wide. In a mild, frost-free, sunny place in the yard, or against a protective, sunny wall, it provides beautiful, open leaves, each cluster like the herringbone skeleton of a fish with tiny leaflets attached to the ribs There are hundreds of small yellow flowers (*see inset*). The topgrowth might die in a cold winter, but new growth should resprout from the ground. Trim for shape after flowering.

OTHER VARIETY *A. dealbata* subsp. *subalpina*.

PLANT PROFILE
HEIGHT 50–100ft (15–30m)
SPREAD 20–30ft (6–10m)
SITE Full sun
SOIL Free-draining
HARDINESS Z9–11 H12–1

Acer campestre Field maple

A

THE TWIN ADVANTAGES of the deciduous field maple are that the five-fingered leaves turn yellow in the autumn before falling, and that it can be heavily pruned and used as a strong, thick hedge. The new spring leaves have a red tinge and obscure the tiny green flowers, while extra color comes from the red fruits in late summer and autumn. The field maple can be grown just about anywhere, from cities to open countryside, in acidic soils or clay.

OTHER VARIETIES *A. campestre* 'Carnival'; *A. campestre* 'Postelense'; *A. campestre* 'Pulverulentum'; *A. campestre* 'Royal Ruby'; *A. campestre* 'Ruby Glow'.

PLANT PROFILE

HEIGHT 50–80ft (15–25m)

SPREAD 25–40ft (8–12m)

SITE Sun or partial shade

SOIL Moist but free-draining, tolerates slight acidity, alkalinity, or clay

HARDINESS Z6–8 H8–4

A | *Acer capillipes* Snakebark maple

THIS IS GROWN FOR ITS SUPERB, highly distinctive, white-striped, gray-green bark and young, red shoots. In the spring there are clusters of small flowers as the new leaves open, followed by green fruits, which gradually redden. With the big autumn flare-up, the leaves turn orange and bright red before falling. In good conditions, it is quite a fast grower, the branches soon arching over.

PLANT PROFILE

HEIGHT 30ft (10m)

SPREAD 30ft (10m)

SITE Sun or partial shade

SOIL Moist but free-draining, tolerates slight acidity

HARDINESS Z5–7 H7–5

Acer cappadocicum 'Aureum' Cappadocian maple

A

THE BRIGHT YELLOW YOUNG LEAVES of this spreading tree, also known as the Caucasian maple, add a vivid, flashy touch in early summer. They turn green over the summer and flare yellow in the autumn before falling. The five- to seven-fingered leaves are quite large, up to 6in (15cm) wide and 4in (10cm) long. The bark is gray and smooth with crinkles.

PLANT PROFILE
HEIGHT 50ft (15m)
SPREAD 30ft (10m)
SITE Sun or partial shade
SOIL Moist but free-draining, tolerates alkalinity and slight acidity
HARDINESS Z5–7 H7–5

OTHER VARIETIES *A. cappadocicum; A. cappadocicum* 'Rubrum'.

Acer davidii 'George Forrest' Père David's maple

THE STREAKED GREEN AND WHITE BARK is the best feature on this deciduous tree, and it really stands out in the winter. Like *Acer capillipes* (*see page 20*), it is also known as snakebark maple. The tiny flowers appear in spring as the red-stalked leaves open; the leaves are up to 8in (20cm) long and dark green, but they barely change color in autumn before falling (for more of a color change, see the varieties below). Growth is open, arching, and spreading.

OTHER VARIETIES   *A. davidii; A. davidii* 'Ernest Wilson'; *A. davidii* 'Rosalie'; *A. davidii* 'Serpentine'.

PLANT PROFILE
HEIGHT 50ft (15m)
SPREAD 50ft (15m)
SITE Sun or partial shade
SOIL Moist but free-draining, tolerates slight acidity
HARDINESS Z5–7 H7–5

Acer griseum Paperbark maple

A

THIS EXTRAORDINARY TREE IS FAMED for its constantly peeling, orange-cinnamon-brown bark (*see inset*). It peels off in thin layers as if it has been badly sunburned. The underlying bark is more fawn-ginger in color. Growth is on the slow side, but as the tree matures, it does spread out. The 4in- (10cm-) long leaves turn from orange to red and scarlet in the autumn before falling. The yellow spring flowers appear as the leaves unfold, and are followed by brown fruits. It makes a superb specimen if you have room.

PLANT PROFILE

HEIGHT 30ft (10m)

SPREAD 30ft (10m)

SITE Sun or partial shade

SOIL Moist but free-draining, tolerates slight acidity

HARDINESS Z4–8 H8–1

A

Acer grosseri var. *hersii* Hers's maple

AN OUTSTANDING MAPLE, this has highly distinctive, fantastically ornamental bark, which is striped white on a green background. The smartly upright growth makes it even more eye-catching. Found in China and introduced in the late 1920s, it is extremely useful in winter gardens, but make sure you remove any shoots that would obscure the bark on the trunk and main branches. Before the leaves fall in the autumn, they turn orange or yellow. Provide shelter from cold winds.

OTHER VARIETY *Acer grosseri* 'Leiden'.

PLANT PROFILE

HEIGHT 50ft (15m)

SPREAD 50ft (15m)

SITE Sun or partial shade

SOIL Moist but free-draining, tolerates slight acidity

HARDINESS Z6–8 H8–6

Acer japonicum 'Aconitifolium' **Full-moon maple**

A

AN UPRIGHT, MULTISTEMMED, bushy, deciduous large shrub or tree, also known as the Japanese maple, grown for its sensational autumn color. The deeply cut leaves turn flame red and give a long show before falling. In spring there is a liberal display of reddish purple flowers, followed by brown fruits. Over summer the leaves are a gentle mid-green. In areas prone to severe winters, place a thick mulch around the base of the trunk (but not touching it) in autumn.

OTHER VARIETIES *A. japonicum; A. japonicum* 'Green Cascade'; *A. japonicum* 'Vitifolium'.

PLANT PROFILE
HEIGHT 15ft (5m)
SPREAD 15ft (5m)
SITE Partial shade
SOIL Moist but free-draining, tolerates slight acidity
HARDINESS Z5–7 H7–5

A

Acer palmatum 'Bloodgood' Japanese maple

THE STRONG-GROWING, UPRIGHT 'BLOODGOOD', whose spread is the same as its height, has foliage that is deep red all summer before turning scarlet in the autumn. It also bears red fruits. Prune young plants in winter, only removing badly placed or crossing shoots to create a nicely arranged display of branches. Shelter from cold winds and late frosts. Avoid soils that can become very dry or very wet; they need to be much the same all year. In areas prone to severe winters, place a thick autumn mulch around the base of the trunk (but not touching it).

OTHER VARIETIES *A. palmatum* f. *atropurpureum*; *A. palmatum* 'Burgundy Lace'; *A. palmatum* 'Moonfire'; *A. palmatum* 'Trompenburg'.

PLANT PROFILE
HEIGHT 15ft (5m)
SPREAD 15ft (5m)
SITE Sun or partial shade
SOIL Moist but free-draining, tolerates slight acidity
HARDINESS Z6–8 H8–4

Acer palmatum 'Ôsakazuki' Japanese maple

A

ONE OF THE STAR MAPLES, 'Ôsakazuki' is highly rated for the way its leaves turn crimson in the autumn before they fall, creating a red carpet around the trunk. Many people think its color is the best of all the maples. The seven-fingered leaves are bright, rich green in summer, and its growth is initially quick. Position where there is shelter from cold winds and late frosts. In areas prone to severe winters, place a thick autumn mulch around the base of the trunk (but not touching it).

OTHER VARIETIES *A. palmatum* var. *heptalobum; A. palmatum* 'Ichigyôji'; *A. palmatum* 'Omurayama'; *A. palmatum* 'Tatsuta'.

PLANT PROFILE
HEIGHT 20ft (6m)
SPREAD 20ft (6m)
SITE Sun or partial shade
SOIL Moist but free-draining, tolerates slight acidity
HARDINESS Z5–8 H8–2

A *Acer palmatum* 'Sango-kaku' **Japanese maple**

ONE OF THE VERY BEST OF THE MAPLES, 'Sango-kaku' has strong, upright growth, and is famed for its new, twiggy shoots, which turn bright red in the winter (*see above, right*). The red really stands out when all the leaves have fallen, and even more so when the yard is covered in snow. The summer leaves are pale green before turning pale orange-yellow in the autumn (*see above, left*).

PLANT PROFILE

HEIGHT 20ft (6m)

SPREAD 15ft (5m)

SITE Sun or partial shade

SOIL Fertile, moist but free-draining, tolerates slight acidity

HARDINESS Z5–8 H8–2

Acer pensylvanicum Moosewood, Striped maple

A

A STRIKING DECIDUOUS MAPLE, *A. pensylvanicum* is widely grown for its attractive green-and-white-striped bark. The young shoots are initially bright green, but they soon darken and bright lines appear. 'Erythrocladum' is an interesting alternative, popular for its eye-catching pink shoots that stand out in winter, especially when lit by the late afternoon sun, and gradually turn orange-red with white stripes. It is not quite as robust as *A. pensylvanicum*, which gets its common name because moose really do chew the wood.

OTHER VARIETY *A. pensylvanicum* 'Erythrocladum'.

PLANT PROFILE
HEIGHT 40ft (12m)
SPREAD 30ft (10m)
SITE Sun or partial shade
SOIL Fertile, moist but free-draining, tolerates slight acidity
HARDINESS Z3–7 H7–1

A

Acer platanoides 'Crimson King' Norway maple

A GIANT, DECIDUOUS, VIGOROUS TREE for a huge garden, the key attraction of 'Crimson King' is the bright red young leaves, turning dark red-purple over the summer. The five-fingered leaves then turn bright yellow in the autumn before falling. In spring, when still leafless, it puts on one of the best flowering displays of any maple when its tiny, red-tinged yellow flowers open. 'Crimson King' tolerates a wide range of soils from alkaline to acidic. Remove crossing or damaged shoots from late autumn to midwinter.

OTHER VARIETIES *A. platanoides* 'Crimson Sentry'; *A. platanoides* 'Faasen's Black'; *A. platanoides* 'Goldsworth Purple'.

PLANT PROFILE
HEIGHT 80ft (25m)
SPREAD 50ft (15m)
SITE Sun or partial shade
SOIL Moist but free-draining, tolerates alkalinity or slight acidity
HARDINESS Z4–7 H7–1

Acer platanoides 'Drummondii' Norway maple

A

THERE IS NO MISTAKING this brightly variegated Norway maple, with its five-fingered leaves, green in the middle and creamy yellow around the edges. Gradually the edges fade to creamy white. If you notice any branches with all-green leaves, promptly remove them. 'Drummondii' tolerates a wide range of soils, from alkaline to acidic. In late autumn or midwinter, cut out crossing or damaged shoots.

PLANT PROFILE
HEIGHT 30–40ft (10–12m)
SPREAD 30–40ft (10–12m)
SITE Sun or partial shade
SOIL Moist but free-draining, tolerates alkalinity or slight acidity
HARDINESS Z3–7 H7–1

A | *Acer pseudoplatanus* 'Brilliantissimum' Planetree maple

THE 100FT- (30M-) TALL *Acer pseudoplatanus* is too large for most
backyards, but the slow-growing, smaller, deciduous 'Brilliantissimum'
can be grown in medium-sized or small yards. It puts on a sensational
spring display when the leaves emerge pink, turn orange and yellow,
and then go white and finally green. The outline of the young tree
also changes from a leafy clump on top of a bare trunk to a fuller
shape. Clusters of tiny spring flowers are followed by green,
sometimes red fruits. It tolerates exposed sites. Prune young plants in
winter to create an attractive arrangement of branches.

OTHER VARIETIES *A. pseudoplatanus* 'Atropurpureum';
A. pseudoplatanus 'Leopoldii'; *A. pseudoplatanus* 'Prinz Handjéry';
A. pseudoplatanus 'Simon-Louis Frères'; *A. pseudoplatanus* 'Worley'.

PLANT PROFILE

HEIGHT 20ft (6m)

SPREAD 25ft (8m)

SITE Sun or partial shade

SOIL Moist but free-draining, slightly acidic to alkaline

HARDINESS Z4–7 H7–1

Acer rubrum 'October Glory' Red maple, Swamp maple

A MAGNIFICENT DECIDUOUS GIANT OF A TREE whose name says it all. The glossy, dark green leaves turn a fantastic bright red in early autumn before falling. In the spring there are clusters of tiny red flowers. For the best autumn color, grow in acidic soil. Prune from late autumn to midwinter to remove any branches that detract from the shape, or are too congested.

OTHER VARIETIES *Acer rubrum; A. rubrum* 'Columnare'; *A. rubrum* RED SUNSET ('Franksred').

A

PLANT PROFILE
HEIGHT 70ft (20m)
SPREAD 30ft (10m)
SITE Sun or partial shade
SOIL Moist but free-draining, preferably acidic
HARDINESS Z3–9 H9–1

A

Acer rufinerve Snakebark maple

TWO GOOD REASONS FOR GROWING the deciduous, arching snakebark maple are its striking bark and its vivid autumn leaves. The former is dark green with white stripes, and stands out sharply in winter when the leaves have fallen (*see inset*). The three-fingered leaves, up to 5in (12cm) long, are dark green before turning orange-yellow and red in autumn. The tiny greenish yellow spring flowers are followed by green fruits with red wings.

OTHER VARIETIES *Acer rufinerve* 'Albolimbatum'; *Acer rufinerve* 'Hatsuyuki'; *Acer rufinerve* 'Winter Gold'.

PLANT PROFILE
HEIGHT 30ft (10m)
SPREAD 30ft (10m)
SITE Sun or partial shade
SOIL Moist but free-draining, tolerates slight acidity
HARDINESS Z6–9 H9–6

Acer saccharum subsp. *nigrum* 'Temple's Upright' Sugar maple

PUTTING ON A TERRIFIC AUTUMN SHOW, the sugar maple's green leaves (with a blue tinge underneath) turn yellow and orange before falling, and with luck might flare crimson. The gray-brown bark becomes furrowed and platelike with age. 'Temple's Upright' makes a narrow, columnar shape, but nurseries don't always stock it; easier to find, and with a much broader spread, is the equally high, 40ft- (12m-) wide, *A. saccharum* (*see inset*).

PLANT PROFILE
HEIGHT 70ft (20m)
SPREAD 15ft (5m)
SITE Sun or partial shade
SOIL Fertile, moist but free-draining, tolerates slight acidity
HARDINESS Z4–8 H8–1

A

Acer shirasawanum 'Aureum' Golden full-moon maple

As WIDE AS IT IS HIGH, 'Aureum' is a good contender for medium-sized yards with its slow, rounded, bushy growth. The leaves are butter yellow through the summer before turning red in the autumn. For the best color, plant 'Aureum' out of direct sun or the leaves will get scorched. The clusters of tiny red-purple spring flowers appear at the same time as the leaves.

PLANT PROFILE
HEIGHT 20ft (6m)
SPREAD 20ft (6m)
SITE Light dappled shade
SOIL Moist but free-draining, tolerates slight acidity
HARDINESS Z5–7 H7–5

OTHER VARIETIES *A. shirasawanum*; *A. shirasawanum* 'Ezo-no-momiji'; *A. shirasawanum* 'Microphyllum'; *A. shirasawanum* 'Palmatifolium'.

Acer tataricum subsp. *ginnala* Amur maple

A

THE THREE-FINGERED LEAVES of this deciduous tree from Japan and China turn deep red in the autumn, providing a much better color effect than its parent, *A. tataricum*. Both are good choices for areas prone to cold winters because they are very hardy. Being slow-growing, subsp. *ginnala* can be grown in medium-sized yards, and is initially more of a large shrub. The small, creamy white, faintly scented flowers are followed by red-winged fruits.

OTHER VARIETY *A. tataricum* subsp. *ginnala* 'Flame'.

PLANT PROFILE
HEIGHT 30ft (10m)
SPREAD 25ft (8m)
SITE Sun or partial shade
SOIL Moist but free-draining, tolerates slight acidity
HARDINESS Z3–7 H7–1

A

Aesculus x *carnea* 'Briotii' Red horse chestnut

WITH ITS GLOSSY LEAVES and large clusters of dark rose-red flowers, the strong-growing, compact 'Briotii' scores higher marks than its parent, *A.* x *carnea*. Its early-summer flowers are followed by spiny fruits. 'Briotii' is a large, spreading deciduous tree, and is suitable only for a good-sized yard. Remove dead, diseased, or crossing branches in winter. 'Plantierensis' is a white-flowering alternative, with a hint of pink.

OTHER VARIETIES *A.* x *carnea* 'Aureomarginata'; *A.* x *carnea* 'Plantierensis'.

PLANT PROFILE
HEIGHT 70ft (20m)
SPREAD 50ft (15m)
SITE Sun or partial shade
SOIL Deep, fertile, moist, and free-draining
HARDINESS Z7–8 H8–7

Aesculus flava Yellow buckeye

A

A GIANT FROM THE EASTERN UNITED STATES, the yellow buckeye makes a terrific sight in parklands. It is impressive enough in summer with its covering of tapered, five-fingered, glossy green leaves (each like a splayed-open hand), but in early autumn the leaves blowtorch into crimson-orange. The tiny yellow flowers appear in clusters up to 7in (18cm) long and are followed by pear-shaped fruits. Remove dead, diseased, or crossing branches in winter.

PLANT PROFILE

HEIGHT 50–80ft (15–25m)

SPREAD 30–50ft (10–15m)

SITE Sun or partial shade

SOIL Deep, fertile, moist but free-draining

HARDINESS Z3–8 H8–1

A

Aesculus x *neglecta* 'Erythroblastos' Sunrise horse chestnut

THE CHIEF REASON FOR GROWING the sunrise horse chestnut is its bright pink new leaf color in the spring. As it matures, the foliage turns whiter and then greenish yellow. Although there are upright clusters of creamy white flowers in midsummer, they are inconspicuous. Smooth-skinned fruits follow the flowers. Promptly remove any dead, diseased, or crossing branches in winter.

PLANT PROFILE

HEIGHT 30ft (10m)

SPREAD 25ft (8m)

SITE Sun or partial shade

SOIL Deep, fertile, moist but free-draining

HARDINESS Z5–8 H8–5

Alnus cordata Italian alder

A

DECIDUOUS, TALL, AND THIN, the Italian alder is wonderfully
impressive in summer. The small leaves are glossy and dark green.
The early-spring catkins, which appear before the leaves, are
followed by small summer fruits. The Italian alder is initially a fast
grower, reaching 50ft (15m) in 15 years (making a highly effective
windbreak), but then grows at a much slower pace. All alders
tolerate poor soil.

PLANT PROFILE
HEIGHT 80ft (25m)
SPREAD 20ft (6m)
SITE Full sun
SOIL Average, moist but free-draining
HARDINESS Z5–7 H7–5

A

Alnus incana 'Aurea' Gray alder

ABOUT HALF THE HEIGHT OF ITS PARENT, *A. incana*, 'Aurea' also puts on fast, deciduous, bushy growth, and is ideal for the kind of terrible soil in which most other trees would wither and die. Unlike most alders, it even tolerates dry conditions. In winter it has orange-red shoots and catkins; the spring buds of the leaves are red, though the young foliage actually emerges yellow before turning pale green. The gray alder makes a tough, vigorous windbreak on poor ground.

OTHER VARIETY *A. incana* 'Laciniata'.

PLANT PROFILE
HEIGHT 30ft (10m)
SPREAD 15ft (5m)
SITE Full sun
SOIL Preferably fertile, moist but free-draining
HARDINESS Z3–7 H7–1

Amelanchier x grandiflora 'Ballerina' Juneberry, Snowy mespilus

AN EXCELLENT DECIDUOUS, SHRUBBY TREE, 'Ballerina' can easily be thinned out in late winter if the growth gets too congested. It has a lively show of spring flowers, which stand out against the new, bronze-tinted leaves. Later, in the autumn, the leaves provide a second striking feature when they turn rich purple-brown, while the copious small fruits turn from red to black and are quickly eaten by birds. The shadbush (*A. canadensis*) is a better choice where space is restricted because it does not spread as much; its autumn leaves turn flashy red and orange.

OTHER VARIETIES *A. x grandiflora* 'Autumn Brilliance'; *A. x grandiflora* 'Robin Hill'; *A. x grandiflora* 'Rubescens'.

PLANT PROFILE	
HEIGHT	20ft (6m)
SPREAD	25ft (8m)
SITE	Sun or partial shade
SOIL	Moist but free-draining, acidic
HARDINESS	Z4–9 H7–1

Amelanchier lamarckii Juneberry, Snowy mespilus

THE JUNEBERRY PUTS ON TWO GOOD SHOWS a year. The first is in spring, when it is liberally covered in clusters of white flowers set against the coppery young leaves. The latter turn dark green over summer, and then comes the autumn show, when they flare red and orange. The flowers are followed by purple-black fruits (edible when cooked), which birds adore. The Juneberry is invariably more multistemmed and shrubby than treelike.

PLANT PROFILE
HEIGHT 30ft (10m)
SPREAD 40ft (12m)
SITE Sun or partial shade
SOIL Moist but free-draining, acidic
HARDINESS Z5–9 H9–5

Aralia elata 'Variegata' Japanese angelica tree

A

AN IRREGULARLY VARIEGATED, DECIDUOUS TREE (with the variegations starting off cream and ending up white), this makes a large, robust plant with huge leaves actually divided into 80 or more leaflets. In autumn the leaves turn yellow before falling. Keep a sharp eye out for new stems with all-green leaves; they must be twisted and ripped off below soil level or the whole tree may lose its variegation. The small, white, late-summer flowers appear in clusters and are followed by tiny black fruits. Provide shelter because harsh winds ruin the leaves; a streambank is an ideal location.

OTHER VARIETIES   *A. elata; A. elata* 'Aureovariegata'.

PLANT PROFILE	
HEIGHT 15ft (5m)	
SPREAD 15ft (5m)	
SITE Sun or partial shade	
SOIL Moist, rich	
HARDINESS Z4–9 H9–1	

A

Araucaria araucana Chilean pine, Monkey puzzle

AN EXTRAORDINARY, EYE-CATCHING, architectural evergreen
conifer, the monkey puzzle needs to be grown in a large lawn
where it can be clearly seen. The trunk is like a vertical pole and has
long, outward-pointing branches with extremely sharp spines at the
tips of the dark green, leathery leaves. It is impossible to know
whether your tree is a male or female until it flowers (an event
which in some cases may never occur). When a female is pollinated,
it produces cones up to 6in (15cm) long. Grow in a sheltered site
away from cold, drying winds.

PLANT PROFILE

HEIGHT 50–80ft (15–25m)

SPREAD 22–30ft (7–10m)

SITE Full sun

SOIL Average, moist but
free-draining

HARDINESS Z7–11 H12–6

Arbutus unedo Strawberry tree

A

AN EXOTIC NAME FOR A SPREADING evergreen tree that produces strawberry-like, warty red fruits in autumn. They ripen from small white flowers that appear the previous autumn, which means that both flowers and fruits appear simultaneously, with striking results. The tree's growth can be on the shrubby side, and the bark is rough, reddish brown, and fissured, but it does not actually peel. The leaves are glossy green. Grow it in a sheltered site and prune, if necessary, in spring.

OTHER VARIETIES *A. unedo* 'Atlantic'; *A. unedo* 'Compacta'; *A. unedo* 'Elfin King'; *A. unedo* 'Quercifolia'; *A. unedo* f. *rubra*.

PLANT PROFILE
HEIGHT 25ft (8m)
SPREAD 25ft (8m)
SITE Full sun
SOIL Rich, free-draining, acidic
HARDINESS Z8–9 H9–6

B | *Betula albosinensis* Chinese red birch

A FIRST-RATE ORNAMENTAL TREE, and one of the best of the birches, the Chinese red birch is grown for its thin, papery, copper-red bark, which peels to expose patches of cream-colored wood beneath. The leaves are on the small side, about 3in (7cm) long, but are an attractive, glossy, deep green before they turn yellow and fall in autumn. The 2½in- (6cm-) long male catkins start forming in the summer, but don't open until the following spring. The Chinese red birch was introduced from China in 1901.

OTHER VARIETIES *B. albosinensis* 'China Ruby'; *B. albosinensis* var. *septentrionalis*.

PLANT PROFILE

HEIGHT 80ft (25m)

SPREAD 30ft (10m)

SITE Full sun or light, dappled shade

SOIL Average, moist but free-draining

HARDINESS Z5–8 H8–5

Betula ermanii Erman's birch

A BEAUTIFUL, DECIDUOUS TREE with an array of upward-pointing branches, Erman's birch's chief asset is its creamy white bark, which keeps peeling in fine strips to expose more patches of white. If the base of the trunk becomes muddy, gently wash it. The glossy green leaves add a light, fluttery touch, and turn yellow in the autumn before falling. Give this tree a prominent position with plenty of room for you to stand back and enjoy it.

OTHER VARIETIES *B. ermanii* 'Grayswood Hill'; *B. ermanii* 'Hakkoda Orange'.

PLANT PROFILE
HEIGHT 70ft (20m)
SPREAD 40ft (12m)
SITE Full sun
SOIL Average, moist but free-draining
HARDINESS Z5–8 H8–5

B | *Betula lenta* Cherry birch, Sweet birch

A LOVELY, DECIDUOUS WOODLAND TREE, the cherry birch has dark red bark, sometimes with a tinge of purple, that turns gray and scaly as it matures. The catkins appear in early spring as the leaves unfold. The tapered, pointed leaves turn yellow in autumn before falling (*see inset*). It is very similar to the yellow birch (*B. alleghaniensis*), though the latter can grow to a towering 80ft (25m) high.

PLANT PROFILE

HEIGHT 50ft (15m)

SPREAD 40ft (12m)

SITE Full sun

SOIL Average, moist but free-draining

HARDINESS Z3–7 H7–2

Betula medwedewii Transcaucasian birch

NOT SO MUCH A TREE as a large, deciduous, slow-growing shrub, this birch has upright, spreading branches, and is very attractive in winter, when it is covered in conspicuous, pointed, glossy buds. The summer leaves are glossy and dark green, before turning yellow and yellow-brown in autumn. The yellow-brown spring catkins are up to 4in (10cm) long, and make a very attractive feature.

PLANT PROFILE
HEIGHT 15ft (5m)
SPREAD 15ft (5m)
SITE Full sun
SOIL Average, moist but free-draining
HARDINESS Z5–7

OTHER VARIETY *B. medwedewii* 'Gold Bark'.

B | *Betula nigra* Black birch, River birch

THE NAME "BLACK BIRCH" is a bit of a misnomer because the shaggy bark is actually reddish brown, and peels off conspicuously in thin layers when young (*see inset*). On mature plants, the bark does become blackish or gray-white, and tends to be cracked. Both male and female catkins appear on the same tree in the spring. The former dangle downward, while the latter are more upright. The glossy green leaves turn yellow before they fall. Remove damaged, diseased, or dead wood in autumn.

OTHER VARIETIES *B. nigra* 'Heritage'; *B. nigra* Wakehurst form.

PLANT PROFILE
HEIGHT 60ft (18m)
SPREAD 40ft (12m)
SITE Sun or partial shade
SOIL Moist but free-draining
HARDINESS Z4–9 H9–1

Betula papyrifera Canoe birch, Paper birch

B

THE HUGE CANOE BIRCH is superb in large yards in winter, when its white bark (spotted with black marks) adds a stunning feature. The attractive bark also peels in paper-thin layers to reveal patches of pinkish orange-brown. The tree is even more distinctive in early spring, when there is a good show of dangling yellow catkins, up to 4in (10cm) long. The dark green, glossy leaves turn a beautiful yellow to orange in the autumn.

PLANT PROFILE

HEIGHT 70ft (20m)

SPREAD 30ft (10m)

SITE Sun or partial shade

SOIL Moist but free-draining

HARDINESS Z2–7 H7–1

OTHER VARIETY *B. papyrifera* 'Vancouver'.

B

Betula pendula 'Tristis' Silver birch

THE WHITE SILVER BIRCH IS A FABULOUS deciduous tree, 'Tristis' being marked by thin, slender, elegant branches with downward-pointing, twiggy growth. The overall effect is of a tall tree that is attractively slight and airy. Silver birches are fast growers, especially when young. Like all white-bark birches, the lower trunk should be pruned of growth so that the white is immediately visible. If it gets splashed with mud, gently sponge clean with warm water. The leaves turn yellow in the autumn.

OTHER VARIETIES *B. pendula* 'Fastigiata'; *B. pendula* 'Golden Beauty'; *B. pendula* 'Laciniata'; *B. pendula* 'Purpurea'.

PLANT PROFILE

HEIGHT 80ft (25m)

SPREAD 30ft (10m)

SITE Full sun

SOIL Moist but free-draining

HARDINESS Z2–7 H7–1

Betula pendula 'Youngii' Young's weeping birch

B

USUALLY DESCRIBED AS MOPHEADED, this deciduous tree has a wide-spreading top, with dangling, weeping growth. The effect is a bit like a small weeping willow (just right for a medium-sized yard), though 'Youngii' also has attractive, peeling white bark. The yellow-brown catkins appear in the spring before the leaves. The latter turn yellow in the autumn before falling.

OTHER VARIETIES *B. pendula* 'Fastigiata'; *B. pendula* 'Golden Beauty'; *B. pendula* 'Laciniata'; *B. pendula* 'Purpurea'.

PLANT PROFILE
HEIGHT 25ft (8m)
SPREAD 30ft (10m)
SITE Full sun
SOIL Moist but free-draining
HARDINESS Z2–7 H7–1

B | *Betula utilis* var. *jacquemontii* Himalayan birch

THIS IS THE BIRCH THE EXPERTS RAVE ABOUT (along with those listed below), and rightly so, because these trees all have astonishing white bark that leaps out at you when the tree is leafless on a sunny winter day. All are extremely tall, while the long, lean branches radiate upward. The effect is even better in early spring, when catkins appear. The dark green leaves turn yellow before they fall in autumn. If the trunk gets splashed with mud, clean with warm water.

OTHER VARIETIES *B. utilis* var. *jacquemontii* 'Doorenbos'; *B. utilis* var. *jacquemontii* 'Grayswood Ghost'; *B. utilis* var. *jacquemontii* 'Inverleith'; *B. utilis* var. *jacquemontii* 'Jermyns'; *B. utilis* var. *jacquemontii* 'Silver Shadow'; *B. utilis* var. *jacquemontii* 'Snowqueen'.

PLANT PROFILE

HEIGHT 60ft (18m)

SPREAD 30ft (10m)

SITE Full sun

SOIL Moist but free-draining

HARDINESS Z4–9 H9–3

Broussonetia papyrifera Paper mulberry

B

THE FAST-GROWING, DECIDUOUS PAPER MULBERRY is a large shrub or multistemmed tree, not to be confused with the mulberry tree (*Morus*). The male and female flowers appear on different trees, and the female trees produce mulberry-like, sweet-tasting, orange-red fruits in autumn. A second attraction is the size of the large, gray-green leaves, which can be 8in (20cm) long. Given a run of hot summers, a young specimen has a chance of achieving treelike stature; cool summers make it more shrublike. Grow in a sheltered site.

PLANT PROFILE	
HEIGHT 25ft (8m)	
SPREAD 25ft (8m)	
SITE Full sun	
SOIL Free-draining	
HARDINESS Z6–9 H9–6	

C

Calocedrus decurrens 'Aureovariegata' Incense cedar

THE VARIEGATED FORM of the evergreen North American incense cedar has occasional, irregular splashes of golden foliage among the sprays of green, needlelike leaves, and adds a gentle rather than a bright, vivid touch. Its critics say it can look diseased, while others love its constant, autumnal-leaf look. If the columnar *C. decurrens* is too tall at a possible 100ft (30m) plus, the medium-sized, slower-growing 'Aureovariegata' is a better bet. The name "incense cedar" refers to the scented, reddish brown bark.

OTHER VARIETY   *C. decurrens* 'Berrima Gold'.

PLANT PROFILE	
HEIGHT 35–50ft (11–15m)	
SPREAD 8–15ft (2.5–5m)	
SITE Sun or partial shade	
SOIL Average, free-draining	
HARDINESS Z5–8 H8–1	

Caragana arborescens 'Walker' Pea tree

C

A SMALL, WEEPING, THORNY TREE, 'Walker' has a short, upright trunk topped with branches that almost immediately start arching downward. They are covered by attractive, small, yellow pealike flowers toward the end of spring. It is a rough, tough kind of plant, and can be grown on open, exposed sites with poor, dry soil. For a larger, shrubbier form, 20ft (6m) high and 12ft (4m) wide, go for *C. arborescens,* which can provide a windbreak or animal-proof barrier. *C. arborescens* 'Lorbergii' is a much more graceful form, with elegant, grasslike leaves, though its flowers are not as big. In all cases, yellow flowers are followed by slender brown pods in the autumn.

OTHER VARIETY *C. arborescens* 'Pendula'.

PLANT PROFILE	
HEIGHT 4–6ft (1.2–2m)	
SPREAD 4–6ft (1.2–2m)	
SITE Full sun	
SOIL Average, free-draining	
HARDINESS Z2–8 H8–1	

C *Carpinus betulus* 'Fastigiata' Hornbeam

THOUGH NOT SUCH A BIG, BEEFY TREE as its parent, *C. betulus*, which reaches 80ft (25m) tall, 'Fastigiata' is still an impressive deciduous specimen. Its shape is a like a gigantic egg, with a thick, congested middle that tapers to a point at the top. Initial growth suggests 'Fastigiata' will be more of a column, but it soon fattens out. There is an attractive display of catkins in the spring, with the females turning into green fruits; another high point comes in the autumn when the leaves turn yellow and then orange before they fall.

OTHER VARIETIES   *C. betulus*; *C. betulus* 'Frans Fontaine'; *C. betulus* 'Pendula'.

PLANT PROFILE
HEIGHT 50ft (15m)
SPREAD 40ft (12m)
SITE Sun or partial shade
SOIL Average, free-draining
HARDINESS Z4–8 H8–3

Carpinus turczaninowii Hornbeam

C

THIS IS A SMALL, ELEGANT, DECIDUOUS TREE, with everything about it on a much more modest scale than the giant common hornbeam (*C. betulus*). Initially its growth is upright, though later it becomes more shrubby and rounded. The leaves are bright red upon opening, then turn glossy, dark green before shading to orange in the autumn and dropping. The female catkins are followed by green fruits, which later turn yellow-brown.

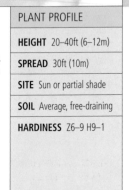

PLANT PROFILE
HEIGHT 20–40ft (6–12m)
SPREAD 30ft (10m)
SITE Sun or partial shade
SOIL Average, free-draining
HARDINESS Z6–9 H9–1

C | *Carya ovata* Shagbark hickory

THIS NORTH AMERICAN TREE is grown for its 8–14in- (20–35cm-) long leaves, which turn from mid-green in summer to vivid golden yellow in autumn before dropping. It is fast growing, with yellow-green male catkins, and the inconspicuous female flowers produce thick-shelled, edible nuts. It needs good soil and shelter to give a quality performance. The shaggy bark, from which it gets its common name, peels off in small, thin, vertical pieces.

PLANT PROFILE
HEIGHT 80ft (25m)
SPREAD 50ft (15m)
SITE Sun or partial shade
SOIL Rich, moist but free-draining
HARDINESS Z4–8 H8–1

Castanea sativa Spanish chestnut, Sweet chestnut

C

A LARGE, LONG-LIVED TREE (there are British specimens about 500 years old), it is tough, vigorous, and almost columnar. It has glossy, dark green, 8in- (20cm-) long leaves that turn yellow, then a wishy-washy brown (occasionally orange) in autumn before falling. The male and female flowers appear on the same tree, followed in autumn by spiny husks containing up to three edible nuts. There are much better trees to grow for ornamental effect, but if you have room for a large woodland tree, why not?

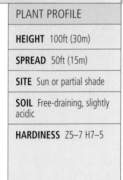

PLANT PROFILE
HEIGHT 100ft (30m)
SPREAD 50ft (15m)
SITE Sun or partial shade
SOIL Free-draining, slightly acidic
HARDINESS Z5–7 H7–5

OTHER VARIETIES *C. sativa* 'Albomarginata'; *C. sativa* 'Heterophylla'; *C. sativa* 'Marron de Lyon'.

C | *Catalpa bignonioides* Indian bean tree, Southern catalpa

THE FAST-GROWING, SHORT-LIVED, DECIDUOUS Indian bean tree actually comes from the southeastern United States. It has vigorous, spreading, multibranched growth, and does not produce one strong, upright, central trunk. The upshot is that you get a terrific canopy of its very large leaves, which are up to 10in (25cm) long. The white summer flowers are 2in (5cm) wide, with yellow and purple-brown blotches in the middle. They are followed by 16in- (40cm-) long, dangling pods that resemble green beans. Plant in an area sheltered from strong winds.

OTHER VARIETIES   *C. bignonioides* 'Aurea'; *C. bignonioides* 'Nana'; *C. bignonioides* 'Variegata'.

PLANT PROFILE
HEIGHT 50ft (15m)
SPREAD 50ft (15m)
SITE Full sun
SOIL Moist but free-draining
HARDINESS Z5–9 H9–5

Catalpa x *erubescens* 'Purpurea' Purple catalpa

C

THE BEST OF THE CATALPAS, 'Purpurea' has astonishing leaves that are
10–16in (25–40cm) long and about 10in (25cm) wide. They are
blackish purple when young, but turn dark green before falling in
autumn. Growth tends to be either upward or spreading outward,
while the late summer flowers (an attraction in their own right) are
dotted or splashed with yellow and purple. They are followed by
slender pods that can reach 16in (40cm) long. Grow in a spot
sheltered from strong winds.

PLANT PROFILE
HEIGHT 50ft (15m)
SPREAD 50ft (15m)
SITE Full sun
SOIL Moist but free-draining
HARDINESS Z5–9 H9–5

C | *Catalpa speciosa* Northern catalpa, Western catalpa

THE DECIDUOUS NORTHERN CATALPA is very similar in appearance
to *C. bignonioides* (*see page 64*). Minor differences are that the leaves
are glossy, dark green, and have slightly longer leaf tips. They turn
yellow from late summer to autumn. The bark is also different, being
gray, scaly, and fissured. And the white flowers open in midsummer,
while those of *C. bignonioides* appear a few weeks later. Slightly
larger, the flowers are also marked with yellow and purple. Grow
with some shelter from strong winds.

PLANT PROFILE
HEIGHT 50ft (15m)
SPREAD 50ft (15m)
SITE Full sun
SOIL Moist but free-draining
HARDINESS Z4–8 H8–1

Cedrus atlantica Glauca Group Blue Atlas cedar

C

YOU WILL NEED A FOOTBALL FIELD to grow this evergreen conifer,
one of the great sights of a large landscaped yard. Growth is initially
slow and conical before it fattens out into a sensational, statuesque
giant with vivid blue–green foliage. Dominating the adjacent area,
it stands out well against a backdrop of bright or dark green trees.
Its cones are up to 3in (8cm) long, and it prefers areas with dry
summers. If there is more than one central growing point, remove
the weaker one.

PLANT PROFILE
HEIGHT To 130ft (40m)
SPREAD To 30ft (10m)
SITE Full sun
SOIL Free-draining
HARDINESS Z6–9 H9–6

OTHER VARIETIES   *C. atlantica*; *C. atlantica* 'Aurea'; *C. atlantica*
'Fastigiata'; *C. atlantica* 'Glauca Pendula'; *C. atlantica* 'Pendula'.

C | *Cedrus deodara* Deodar cedar

A GIANT OF AN EVERGREEN CONIFER, with a drooping central stem, the Deodar cedar comes from northwest Pakistan. Initial growth is fast, and the leaves are like little needles about 2in (5cm) long. They are grayish blue when young, turning deep green. The autumn flowers later yield 3–5in- (8–12cm-) long cones, which start off green but mature to purple-brown.

PLANT PROFILE	
HEIGHT To 130ft (40m)	
SPREAD To 30ft (10m)	
SITE Full sun	
SOIL Free-draining	
HARDINESS Z6–9 H9–6	

OTHER VARIETIES *C. deodara* 'Aurea'; *C. deodara* 'Feelin' Blue'; *C. deodara* 'Golden Horizon'; *C. deodara* 'Karl Fuchs'; *C. deodara* 'Pendula'; *C. deodara* 'Roman Candle'.

Cedrus libani 'Sargentii' Cedar of Lebanon

C

FORGET ITS PARENT, which grows to a gigantic 100ft (30m) high and wide, because this is a slow-growing mini-cedar that wants to flop on the ground. If you train one of its stems against a vertical cane, it can become an upright, weeping mound of bluish green, needlelike leaves. It adds variety to a group of tall, thin, and small rounded conifers, and can also be grown by a rock garden, but not within it, because it is far too big. 'Sargentii' is also useful in Japanese-style gardens where the larger landscape is scaled down.

PLANT PROFILE
HEIGHT 2½–5ft (0.6–1.5m)
SPREAD 5–10ft (1.5–3m)
SITE Full sun
SOIL Free-draining, tolerates alkalinity
HARDINESS Z7–9 H9–7

C | *Celtis australis* Southern nettle tree

A MASSIVE DECIDUOUS TREE for only the largest of yards, the southern nettle tree has a sturdy, vertical trunk and a billowing mass of leaves, each up to 6in (15cm) long. The small spring flowers are followed by rounded, edible, berrylike fruits, which turn from red to blackish brown when ripe. In the wild, this tree grows in southwest Asia and southern Europe.

PLANT PROFILE

HEIGHT 70ft (20m)

SPREAD 70ft (20m)

SITE Sun or partial shade

SOIL Fairly dry, free-draining

HARDINESS Z6–8 H8–6

Cephalotaxus harringtonii Cowtail pine, Plum yew

SOMETIMES STILL KNOWN as *C. harringtonia*, not *harringtonii*, this is an evergreen coniferous shrub that, with luck, can occasionally make a small tree. It is ideal for hedging. The brown bark tends to flake, while the creamy white flowers are followed by 1in- (2.5cm-) long, olive green fruits. In a cool, moist climate, place it in full sun. When it is being grown in partial shade, the soil should be moist and free-draining. Although it tolerates a wide range of soils, it does need shelter from cold, drying winds. You can trim hedges in early summer, as hard as you wish, without any ill effects.

OTHER VARIETY   *C. harringtonii* 'Fastigiata'.

PLANT PROFILE
HEIGHT 10–30ft (3–10m)
SPREAD 10–20ft (3–6m)
SITE Sun or partial shade
SOIL Fertile, moist but free-draining
HARDINESS Z6–9 H9–6

C

Cercidiphyllum japonicum Katsura tree

THE BEST REASON FOR GROWING this modest-looking tree is that when the leaves turn yellow, orange, and red in autumn before they fall, they release a delicious, potent scent of burned sugar, which is immediately detectable from 20ft (6m) away. Growth is multistemmed and bushy, and fast in good conditions. The tiny, red, petal-less flowers open at the same time as the leaves, or just before them, with males and females appearing on separate trees. Acidic ground provides better autumn colors. Shelter from cold winds, possibly in a woodland setting. *C. japonicum* f. *pendulum* (*see inset*) is much slower growing than its parent and has more graceful, arching branches.

OTHER VARIETIES *C. japonicum* f. *pendulum; C. japonicum* 'Rotfuchs'; *C. japonicum* 'Strawberry'.

PLANT PROFILE
HEIGHT 70ft (20m)
SPREAD 50ft (15m)
SITE Sun or dappled shade
SOIL Deep, rich, moist but free-draining, preferably acidic
HARDINESS Z4–8 H8–1

Cercidiphyllum magnificum Weeping Katsura tree

C

MAKING A SMALLER TREE than *C. japonicum* (*see opposite*), *C. magnificum* has larger leaves. They are still not huge, at 5in (12cm) long, but they do provide a bit more color in autumn. It is often still listed as *C. japonicum* var. *magnificum*. Plant in acidic soil for even stronger autumn colors, and make sure the tree is sheltered from cold winds.

OTHER VARIETIES *C. japonicum* 'Rotfuchs'; *C. japonicum* 'Strawberry'.

PLANT PROFILE
HEIGHT 30ft (10m)
SPREAD 25ft (8m)
SITE Sun or dappled shade
SOIL Deep, rich, moist but free-draining, preferably acidic
HARDINESS Z4–8

C *Cercis canadensis* Eastern redbud

A SPREADING, OFTEN MULTISTEMMED, DECIDUOUS TREE, the eastern redbud gives a good display of color in spring and autumn. When its leaves unfold, they are bronze, turning bright green over summer and then yellow in autumn. The flowers (*see inset*) are small and beautiful, appearing on the bare stems before the leaves unfold. Blooms vary in color from crimson to pink, purple, and white. They are followed by seed pods, which turn from green to brown when ripe. To produce larger leaves, cut branches back hard to the main trunk in early spring. New, spindly growth will soon appear. Avoid transplanting this tree.

OTHER VARIETIES *C. canadensis* 'Forest Pansy'; *C. canadensis* var. *occidentalis.*

PLANT PROFILE
HEIGHT 30ft (10m)
SPREAD 30ft (10m)
SITE Full sun or dappled shade
SOIL Rich, moist but free-draining
HARDINESS Z4–9 H9–2

Cercis chinensis Chinese redbud

C

A DENSE, DECIDUOUS SHRUB OR SMALL TREE from central China, the Chinese redbud has glossy, leathery, rich green leaves about 5in (12cm) long. There is a good end-of-spring display of pinkish flowers in clusters (*see inset*) before the leaves appear. To produce larger leaves, cut branches back hard to the main trunk in early spring. New, spindly growth will soon appear as a result. Like the eastern redbud, this tree hates being moved.

OTHER VARIETY *C. chinensis* 'Avondale'.

PLANT PROFILE
HEIGHT 20ft (6m)
SPREAD 15ft (5m)
SITE Full sun or dappled shade
SOIL Rich, moist but free-draining
HARDINESS Z6–9 H9–3

C

Cercis siliquastrum Judas tree

AN EXTREMELY ATTRACTIVE, SEE-THROUGH DECIDUOUS TREE, the Judas tree produces several thick stems that snake upward and are covered with heart- to kidney-shaped leaves. The leaves are bronze when young, then turn blue-green over the summer, and end up yellow in autumn. The flowers are a beautiful, rich magenta to pink, and look like they have been glued onto the bare branches. They are followed by long, flat pods, which turn from pink to brown. Like the other cercis trees, it hates being disturbed.

OTHER VARIETIES   *C. siliquastrum* f. *albida*; *C. siliquastrum* 'Bodnant'.

PLANT PROFILE

HEIGHT 30ft (10m)

SPREAD 30ft (10m)

SITE Full sun or dappled shade

SOIL Rich, moist but free-draining

HARDINESS Z6–9 H9–5

Chamaecyparis lawsoniana 'Ellwoodii' Lawson cypress

C

'ELLWOODII' MAKES A THICK, CHUNKY, EVERGREEN column of several upright stems. Growth is tightly packed, dense, and slightly conical, being fuller at the base and middle than the top, where it tapers to a point. It is slow-growing, reaching only 6ft (2m) after ten years, but eventually reaching four times that. The new leaves are blue-gray before turning gray-green and then bluish in winter. Avoid exposed sites. Trim trees grown as hedges from an early age, but do not cut into old wood or you will be left with bare patches.

OTHER VARIETY *C. lawsoniana* 'Ellwood's Gold'.

PLANT PROFILE
HEIGHT 22ft (7m)
SPREAD 5ft (1.5m)
SITE Full sun
SOIL Free-draining, slightly acidic
HARDINESS Z5–9 H9–5

C

Chamaecyparis lawsoniana 'Green Pillar' Lawson cypress

A SHAPELY, TALL AND THIN ARCHITECTURAL PLANT, 'Green Pillar' will reach above head height after ten years and will eventually make a much taller tree with rich green leaves. It forms a lively color contrast with golden yellow cypresses, such as 'Golden Pot' and 'Golden Wonder', and the popular 'Columnaris', which is an evergreen pillar of pale blue-gray. Both 'Columnaris' and 'Green Pillar' are highly rated by garden designers for their eye-catching, vertical shape. When trimming any of these cypresses, do so from early spring to autumn, but do not cut into old wood or you will be left with bare, brown, woody patches.

OTHER VARIETIES *C. lawsoniana* 'Columnaris'; *C. lawsoniana* 'Fraseri'; *C. lawsoniana* 'Stardust'.

PLANT PROFILE
HEIGHT 30ft (10m)
SPREAD 6ft (2m)
SITE Full sun
SOIL Moist but free-draining, preferably acidic but tolerates alkalinity
HARDINESS Z5–9 H9–5

Chamaecyparis lawsoniana 'Pembury Blue' Lawson cypress

C

ONE OF THE BEST of the bright blue-gray Lawson cypresses, 'Pembury Blue' makes a large, solid, conical, evergreen shape. The silver-blue color is most striking on the new growth, making a lively contrast with a background of green trees. It is a good choice for a boundary "wall" of mixed Lawson cypresses, with thin uprights and chunky, solid tall growers.

OTHER VARIETY *C. lawsoniana* 'Spek'.

PLANT PROFILE
HEIGHT 50ft (15m)
SPREAD 10ft (3m)
SITE Full sun
SOIL Moist but free-draining, preferably acidic but tolerates alkalinity
HARDINESS Z5–9 H9–5

Chamaecyparis nootkatensis 'Pendula' Nootka cypress

A WONDERFULLY SHAGGY EVERGREEN CONIFER from northwestern North America, with arching branches and dangling, dark green leaves, it often makes a witchlike shape, which can be spiced up with just a little judicious pruning, emphasizing its arms and head. The spring flowers are followed by small, round cones. Some clones have more compact, dense growth. It prefers slightly acidic soil, though it also tolerates dry, alkaline ground. Regular pruning is not necessary, since it has a good natural shape.

PLANT PROFILE

HEIGHT 100ft (30m)

SPREAD 25ft (8m)

SITE Full sun

SOIL Moist but free-draining

HARDINESS Z4–7 H7–1

Chamaecyparis obtusa 'Tetragona Aurea' Hinoki cypress

C

IF YOU GROW THIS EVERGREEN (introduced about 130 years ago) in full sun, you will get golden yellow to bronze-yellow leaves, but in shade the color ends up being much greener. Its shape is slightly blobby and irregular (unlike those conifers that form smooth-sided, neatly shaped cones), thanks to the sparse, wide-spreading branches. Eventually it becomes quite bushy and upright, making an impressive specimen tree. It prefers slightly acidic soil, but tolerates alkaline conditions. Regular pruning is not necessary.

OTHER VARIETIES *C. obtusa* 'Crippsii'; *C. obtusa* 'Goldilocks'.

PLANT PROFILE
HEIGHT 30ft (10m)
SPREAD 10ft (3m)
SITE Full sun
SOIL Moist but free-draining
HARDINESS Z4–8 H8–1

C

Chamaecyparis pisifera 'Boulevard' Sawara cypress

THIS IS A BIG-SELLING, HIGHLY POPULAR evergreen cypress because of its soft blue-green leaves and loosely conical shape, which can easily be sharpened up. A row of 'Boulevard' can be grown as a hedge, or a single one can be used with other differently shaped and colored cypresses in a mixed planting. The spring flowers are followed by minuscule cones (*pisifera* means "pealike"), which turn from green to brown as they mature. Regular pruning is not needed.

OTHER VARIETY *C. pisifera* 'Curly Tops'.

PLANT PROFILE
HEIGHT 30ft (10m)
SPREAD 8ft (2.5m)
SITE Full sun
SOIL Moist, slightly acidic
HARDINESS Z4–8 H8–1

Chamaecyparis pisifera 'Filifera Aurea' Sawara cypress

C

IT MIGHT REACH 40FT (12M) HIGH, but is initially very slow-growing, and is easily kept small and neat looking with judicious pruning (otherwise it can get quite ragged). Its golden yellow leaves benefit from being highlighted against a dark green background. The spring flowers are followed by tiny cones, which turn from green to brown.

PLANT PROFILE
HEIGHT 40ft (12m)
SPREAD 25ft (8m)
SITE Full sun
SOIL Moist, slightly acidic
HARDINESS Z4–8 H8–1

OTHER VARIETY *C. pisifera* 'Sungold'.

C | *Cladrastis kentukea* Yellowwood

A DECIDUOUS, SPREADING TREE from the southeastern United States, the yellowwood has two main advantages. In late spring, there are faintly scented white flowers with yellow marks, up to 1¼in (3cm) long, and in the autumn, the bright green leaves turn yellow before falling. To get these two good shows, it must be grown in an open position where it is not exposed to strong winds, and the summers should ideally be long and hot.

OTHER VARIETY *C. kentukea* 'Rosea'.

PLANT PROFILE
HEIGHT 40ft (12m)
SPREAD 30ft (10m)
SITE Full sun
SOIL Free-draining
HARDINESS Z4–9 H9–1

Cornus alternifolia 'Argentea' Green osier, Pagoda dogwood

C

MORE OF A HUGE, DECIDUOUS, MULTISTEMMED SHRUB than a tree, the pagoda dogwood is grown for its good show of spreading, tiered branches and the way in which the white-margined leaves burn red and purple in autumn. The flattened clusters of white, early-summer flowers are followed by round, blue-black fruits. It is an excellent choice for a wild or cottage garden. In the wild, on the eastern side of North America, it is found growing by streams in woods and thickets.

PLANT PROFILE

HEIGHT 10ft (3m)

SPREAD 8ft (2.5m)

SITE Full sun or partial shade

SOIL Moist but free-draining

HARDINESS Z4–8 H8–1

C | *Cornus controversa* 'Variegata' Giant dogwood

A HIGHLY RATED, SLOW-GROWING DECIDUOUS TREE, this dogwood has attractively layered horizontal branches covered with bright green-and-white variegated leaves. Two extra plus points are the spring show of white flowers, followed by round, blue-black fruits, and the autumn leaf flare-up, when the foliage turns rich red and purple before falling.

PLANT PROFILE

HEIGHT 25ft (8m)

SPREAD 25ft (8m)

SITE Full sun or partial shade

SOIL Moist but free-draining, neutral to acidic

HARDINESS Z6–9 H9–6

Cornus 'Eddie's White Wonder' Dogwood

C

ONE OF THE VERY BEST DOGWOODS, 'Eddie's White Wonder' has a compact, upright shape and a good show in spring and autumn. In spring there is a highly conspicuous display of rounded, white, petal-like growths (called bracts), up to 3in (8cm) long, which surround the purple-green flowers. The long, tapering leaves provide color in the autumn, when they turn orange, red, and purple before falling. It makes a conical tree or a multistemmed shrub that is very slow-growing, reaching about 8ft (2.5m) high after ten years.

PLANT PROFILE
HEIGHT 20ft (6m)
SPREAD 15ft (5m)
SITE Full sun or partial shade
SOIL Moist but free-draining, neutral to acidic
HARDINESS Z5–8 H8–5

C | *Cornus florida* 'Cherokee Chief' Flowering dogwood

THE FLOWER BUDS ARE EVIDENT ALL THROUGH WINTER, covered by beautiful, rich pink, petal-like growths (or bracts), which do not open until late spring. They make a display that is worth waiting for. The 6in- (15cm-) long leaves give a second show when they turn red and purple in the autumn. The overall shape is like a large shrub or small tree.

OTHER VARIETIES *C. florida* 'Cherokee Princess'; *C. florida* 'Cloud Nine'; *C. florida* RAINBOW ('Marzelli'); *C. florida* 'Red Giant'; *C. florida* f. *rubra*; *C. florida* 'Spring Song'; *C. florida* 'Sunset'.

PLANT PROFILE
HEIGHT 20ft (6m)
SPREAD 25ft (8m)
SITE Full sun or parrtial shade
SOIL Moist but free-draining
HARDINESS Z5–8 H8–3

Cornus kousa var. *chinensis* Dogwood

C

A SUPERB DECIDUOUS TREE WHOSE DARK GREEN LEAVES turn a beautiful deep crimson-purple in autumn when they fall. Initially growth is conical, though it tends to spread more with age. The flowers are small and green, and are surrounded by vivid white, petal-like bracts which turn reddish pink. They are followed by strawberry-like, fleshy red fruits. This dogwood needs to be shown off on a large lawn. Avoid growing it in alkaline soil.

OTHER VARIETIES *C. kousa*; *C. kousa* var. *chinensis* 'China Girl'; *C. kousa* 'Gold Star'.

PLANT PROFILE
HEIGHT 22ft (7m)
SPREAD 15ft (5m)
SITE Full sun or partial shade
SOIL Deep, rich, free-draining, acidic
HARDINESS Z5–8 H8–5

C | *Cornus kousa* 'Satomi' Dogwood

THIS RELATIVELY RECENT INTRODUCTION FROM JAPAN can be called either a large shrub or a small tree, and really stands out in early summer, when it is covered with dark, rich pink, petal-like bracts, which surround the tiny flower heads. There is a second show in autumn, when the foliage turns a highly satisfying, dark red-purple before falling. It needs to be shown off on a large lawn. Avoid growing this dogwood in alkaline soil.

OTHER VARIETIES *C. kousa.*

PLANT PROFILE

HEIGHT 22ft (7m)

SPREAD 15ft (5m)

SITE Full sun or partial shade

SOIL Deep, rich, free-draining, slightly acidic

HARDINESS Z5–8 H8–5

Cornus nuttallii Pacific dogwood

C

VIGOROUS AND TALL, THE DECIDUOUS PACIFIC DOGWOOD has one, or possibly two, seasons of interest. In late spring, the small purple and green flowers are surrounded by highly distinctive, white or pink-tinged petal-like bracts (*see inset*), and in autumn the large leaves sometimes turn red. The spring flowers are followed by small, round, orange-red fruits. Do not confuse this large dogwood, which needs plenty of space, with the much shorter kinds.

OTHER VARIETIES *C. nuttallii* 'Ascona'; *C. nuttallii* 'Gold Spot'; *C. nuttallii* 'Monarch'; *C. nuttallii* 'Portlemouth'.

PLANT PROFILE
HEIGHT 40ft (12m)
SPREAD 25ft (8m)
SITE Full sun or partial shade
SOIL Moist but free-draining
HARDINESS Z7–8 H8–7

C *Corylus avellana* Hazel

THE DECIDUOUS HAZEL IS BEST KNOWN for its dangling yellowish catkins, up to 2½in (6cm) long. They are followed by broad green leaves that cover the whole shrubby tree. Look carefully again in late summer and you will see the lime green cobnuts. Hazels are often incorporated into mixed "tapestry" hedges, and can be restricted to about 10ft (3m) high by spring pruning. They survive hard pruning or even coppicing. Male catkins and female flowers appear on the same plant. *C. avellana* 'Contorta' (*see inset*) has striking, twisted shoots that look their best in winter.

OTHER VARIETIES *C. avellana* 'Aurea'; *C. avellana* 'Cosford Cob'; *C. avellana* 'Heterophylla'; *C. avellana* 'Webb's Prize Cobb'.

PLANT PROFILE	
HEIGHT	15ft (5m)
SPREAD	15ft (5m)
SITE	Sun or partial shade
SOIL	Free-draining
HARDINESS	Z4–8

Corylus colurna Turkish hazel

C

A SPLENDID DECIDUOUS TREE, the Turkish hazel is increasingly found in cities. Interest kicks off in late winter, when it produces yellow catkins, about 2½in (6cm) long, dangling from the bare branches. Over the summer, the tree assumes a lovely conical shape of dark green leaves, and in autumn there are plenty of edible nuts. The leaves then turn yellow before they fall. It is a good tree for a modest arboretum.

PLANT PROFILE
HEIGHT 70ft (20m)
SPREAD 22ft (7m)
SITE Sun or partial shade
SOIL Free-draining, tolerates alkalinity
HARDINESS Z5–7 H7–5

C | *Cotinus* 'Grace' Smoke bush

THE BEST REASON FOR CHOOSING the fast-growing, deciduous 'Grace' is for the great autumn show, when the leaves turn bright red. When this bushy, vigorous small tree or large shrub is covered in soft, purple-red leaves and has reached its full height, it is absolutely exhilarating. Although the flowers are initially minuscule, they turn into plumes up to 8in (20cm) long in hot summers, resembling wafting puffs of smoke—hence the common name. Prune hard each spring for large leaves.

OTHER VARIETY *C.* 'Flame'.

PLANT PROFILE

HEIGHT 20ft (6m)

SPREAD 15ft (5m)

SITE Full sun or partial shade

SOIL Average, moist but free-draining

HARDINESS Z5–8 H8–5

Cotoneaster frigidus 'Cornubia'

C

A GIANT OF A SHRUBBY TREE, with arching branches, 'Cornubia' is evergreen in mild areas, otherwise dropping some leaves. Many of the leaves turn bronze over winter. Growth is vigorous, and the clusters of red fruits are about the largest to be found on a tall cotoneaster. They give a bright, punchy show through autumn into winter, ending only when hungry birds strip them off. The fruit is preceded by white summer flowers. This tree is still sometimes known as *C.* 'Cornubia'.

OTHER VARIETIES *C. frigidus* 'Fructu Luteo'; *C. frigidus* 'Notcutt's Variety'; *C. frigidus* 'Pershore Coral'.

PLANT PROFILE
HEIGHT 20ft (6m)
SPREAD 20ft (6m)
SITE Full sun or partial shade
SOIL Average, free-draining
HARDINESS Z7–8 H8–7

C   *Crataegus laevigata* 'Rosea Flore Pleno' Hawthorn

MOST HAWTHORNS ARE TALL TREES, about 20ft (6m) high, but two kinds (this and *C. monogyna, see opposite*) can be grown as thorny, impenetrable, deciduous hedges. 'Rosea Flore Pleno' puts on a lovely early summer show with its double, pink scented flowers, later followed by red fruits or "haws." Grow it with 'Crimson Cloud', which has bright red flowers, 'Paul's Scarlet', with dark pink flowers, and 'Plena', with double white flowers. They create a gorgeous show. The best time for trimming is in the summer, post-flowering, but you will lose the fruits. For a mixed hedge, grow it with beech, cotoneaster, holly, hornbeam, honeysuckle, and viburnum.

OTHER VARIETIES   *C. laevigata* 'Crimson Cloud'; *C. laevigata* 'Paul's Scarlet'; *C. laevigata* 'Plena'.

PLANT PROFILE
HEIGHT 18ft (5.5m)
SPREAD 18ft (5.5m)
SITE Full sun or partial shade
SOIL Any, except waterlogged
HARDINESS Z5–8 H8–4

Crataegus monogyna Singleseed hawthorn

C

HAWTHORN IS OFTEN SEEN GROWING IN ENGLISH HEDGEROWS, where it bursts into flower at the end of spring, being covered by clusters of small, white, scented blooms (*see inset*). They are followed by shiny, dark red fruits. Singleseed hawthorn can be trimmed for size after flowering or in autumn. It is rough and tough, and survives the worst you or the weather can throw at it. The fruit is edible, but by all accounts, hardly anyone goes back for more.

OTHER VARIETIES   *C. monogyna* 'Biflora'; *C. monogyna* 'Stricta'; *C. monogyna* 'Variegata'.

PLANT PROFILE
HEIGHT 30ft (10m)
SPREAD 25ft (8m)
SITE Full sun or partial shade
SOIL Any, except waterlogged
HARDINESS Z5–7 H7–5

C | *Crataegus persimilis* 'Prunifolia' Hawthorn

IN WINTER THIS HAWTHORN IS NOTHING SPECIAL, being a mass of twigs and dense leafless growth, but in the spring it starts breaking out in dark green leaves up to 3in (8cm) long. The early summer flowers provide a decent show of small white blooms, but most people grow it for the autumn show, when you get bright red fruits and leaves that quickly turn flashy yellow, orange, and red. It is impressive growing on a large lawn, or along the edge of the yard.

OTHER VARIETY   *C. persimilis* 'Prunifolia Splendens'.

PLANT PROFILE
HEIGHT 25ft (8m)
SPREAD 30ft (10m)
SITE Full sun or partial shade
SOIL Any, except waterlogged
HARDINESS Z6–7

Cryptomeria japonica 'Sekkan-sugi' Japanese cedar

C

THE JAPANESE CEDARS ARE RELATED TO the giant redwoods, and have the same kind of thick, spongy, fibrous, orange-tinted bark. They are evergreen conifers with some extreme forms, such as the shrubby 6ft- (2m-) high 'Bandai-sugi', and the 12ft- (4m-) high narrow column of 'Pyramidata'. 'Sekkan-sugi' is moderately slow-growing with creamy yellow leaves, which turn almost white in winter. The Japanese cedar is one of the few conifers that can be coppiced, by cutting back growth to 12in (30cm) from the ground in spring.

OTHER VARIETIES *C. japonica* Elegans Group; *C. japonica* 'Spiralis'.

PLANT PROFILE
HEIGHT 30ft (10m)
SPREAD 20ft (6m)
SITE Full sun or partial shade
SOIL Deep, rich, free-draining, tolerates alkalinity
HARDINESS Z6–9 H9–6

C

Cunninghamia lanceolata China fir

A MAGNIFICENTLY IMPRESSIVE AND VERY CURIOUS evergreen conifer, the China fir looks like a bit of a hybrid. It is closely related to the redwoods, and has the same kind of thick, fibrous, rust-colored bark, while the sharp-tipped leaves look a bit like those of the monkey puzzle (*Araucaria araucana, see page 46*). The flowers are followed by 1½in- (4cm-) long cones. Do not try to banish the China fir to the farthest part of the yard; it needs to go center stage with shelter from the wind.

OTHER VARIETY *C. lanceolata* 'Bánó'.

PLANT PROFILE
HEIGHT 70ft (20m)
SPREAD 20ft (6m)
SITE Full sun or dappled shade
SOIL Moist but free-draining
HARDINESS Z7–9 H9–7

x *Cupressocyparis leylandii* 'Castlewellan' Leyland cypress

C

GIVEN A CHANCE TO SHOOT UP and up in a large area where it can grow without plunging the neighbors' yard into permanent twilight, the fast-growing 'Castlewellan' makes a sensational evergreen conifer with sprays of yellow foliage. When it is grown beside x *C. leylandii* in a hedge, you get a nice mix of different colors. You can stop it at hedge height by trimming it two or three times over spring and summer, slowing it down and keeping it at about 6ft (2m). Do not cut into old wood because it will not resprout.

OTHER VARIETIES x *C. leylandii* 'Gold Rider'; x *C. leylandii* 'Herculea'; x *C. leylandii* 'Olive's Green'; x *C. leylandii* 'Robinson's Gold'.

PLANT PROFILE
HEIGHT 80ft (25m)
SPREAD To 15ft (5m)
SITE Full sun or partial shade
SOIL Deep, well-drained
HARDINESS Z6–9 H9–3

C | *Cupressus arizonica* var. *glabra* 'Blue Ice' Smooth cypress

AN EXTRAORDINARY EVERGREEN CONIFER, this cypress makes a fairly dense column of upright growth. Though it can end up high in the sky, it is a relatively slow grower, putting on 10ft (3m) in its first 10 years, and its blue–gray or silver leaves are highly rated. It is quite happy in hot, dry conditions, but shelter from cold, drying winds is important. If you are giving it a trim, do so in late spring, but do not cut back into old wood because it will not resprout.

OTHER VARIETIES *C. arizonica* var. *glabra* 'Aurea'; *C. arizonica* var. *glabra* 'Fastigiata'; *C. arizonica* 'Pyramidalis'.

PLANT PROFILE
HEIGHT 70ft (20m)
SPREAD 10ft (3m)
SITE Full sun
SOIL Free-draining, tolerates alkalinity
HARDINESS Z7–9

Cupressus macrocarpa 'Goldcrest' Monterey cypress

C

A SUPERB, NARROW, GOLDEN YELLOW EVERGREEN CONIFER, the Monterey cypress makes a vivid sight against a dark green background. Growth is tightly packed, helping to make it an attractive and effective hedge or screen. If possible, provide hot, dry conditions, with shelter from cold, drying winds. If you need to prune it, do so in late spring, but do not cut back into old, bare wood because it will not resprout.

OTHER VARIETIES *C. macrocarpa* 'Donard Gold'; *C. macrocarpa* 'Golden Pillar'; *C. macrocarpa* 'Golden Spire'; *C. macrocarpa* 'Wilma'.

PLANT PROFILE
HEIGHT 16ft (5m)
SPREAD 8ft (2.5m)
SITE Full sun
SOIL Free-draining, tolerates alkalinity
HARDINESS Z7–11 H12–7

C

Cydonia oblonga 'Vranja' Quince

TO PERSUADE A DECIDUOUS QUINCE—which is completely different from flowering quince (*Chaenomeles*)—to fruit, it needs to be grown in a mild region or against a sheltered wall to prevent the flowers from being damaged by frost. The young fruits then need a long, hot summer to ripen. 'Vranja' scores over its parent, *C. oblonga,* because it has scented, pale green, pearlike fruits, which ripen to golden yellow. They are used for flavoring and in preserves, but need cooking before they can be eaten. Prune lightly in late winter for an open framework, and to remove any dead wood.

OTHER VARIETIES *C. oblonga* 'Lusitanica'; *C. oblonga* 'Meech's Prolific'.

PLANT PROFILE
HEIGHT 15ft (5m)
SPREAD 15ft (5m)
SITE Full sun
SOIL Fertile, moist but free-draining
HARDINESS Z5–9 H9–5

Davidia involucrata Dove tree, Handkerchief tree

D

A HIGHLY RATED DECIDUOUS TREE from China, much loved by experts, it catches the eye in late spring when its small flowers are surrounded by showy, white, petal-like bracts, which look like handkerchiefs from a distance. It is so impressive it needs to be given a prominent position in the yard. In summer, the spreading branches are covered by leaves up to 6in (15cm) long, with soft hairs underneath. In the autumn it bears small green fruits that gradually turn purple-brown. The orange-brown bark is another attraction, gradually peeling off in flakes.

OTHER VARIETY *D. involucrata* var. *vilmoriniana.*

PLANT PROFILE
HEIGHT 50ft (15m)
SPREAD 30ft (10m)
SITE Sun or partial shade
SOIL Fertile, moist but free-draining
HARDINESS Z6–8 H8–6

D | *Diospyros kaki* Chinese persimmon, Japanese persimmon

THIS IS A FUN TREE, with most of the action happening in the autumn. The glossy, dark green leaves, which are quite large, at up to 8in (20cm) long, turn yellow, orange-red, and purple, giving a lively show before falling. And the female plants produce fruits (a nearby male is usually necessary, and certainly provides a better crop), which follow the small, bell-shaped, pale yellow flowers. The fruits (*see inset*) are initially yellow (when they taste bitter), ripening to orange, but although they are juicy, most people find them crammed with too many seeds. Provide a warm, sunny, sheltered site to avoid cold winds and late frosts.

OTHER VARIETY *D. lotus.*

PLANT PROFILE
HEIGHT 30ft (10m)
SPREAD 22ft (7m)
SITE Full sun
SOIL Deep, fertile, free-draining
HARDINESS Z7–10 H10–7

Drimys winteri Winter's bark

D

AN EXTREMELY ATTRACTIVE SOUTH AMERICAN TREE, Winter's bark has many interesting features but does need a mild, sheltered, frost-free garden. Given the right conditions, it will produce masses of small, white, faintly scented flowers in clusters at the start of summer, but trees might have to be at least ten years old before that happens. The dark green, tactile leaves (bluish white beneath) provide extra interest over summer, being leathery and up to 8in (20cm) long. The gray bark is aromatic.

OTHER VARIETIES *D. winteri* var. *andina; D. winteri* var. *chilensis.*

PLANT PROFILE
HEIGHT 50ft (15m)
SPREAD 30ft (10m)
SITE Sun or partial shade
SOIL Fertile, moist but free-draining
HARDINESS Z8–11 H12–8

E *Elaeagnus umbellata* Autumn olive

MAKING A LARGE, DECIDUOUS, VIGOROUS SHRUB or a small tree, this is highly rated for its leaves, which start off silvery before turning bright green. The scented flowers are small and white, appearing in late spring, and are followed in autumn by a good show of small, round, silvery fruits that turn red when ripe. It makes a good choice for a wide space at the back of a large border.

PLANT PROFILE
HEIGHT 15ft (5m)
SPREAD 15ft (5m)
SITE Full sun
SOIL Fertile, free-draining
HARDINESS Z4–8 H8–1

Emmenopterys henryi

THIS RARELY SEEN DECIDUOUS TREE from the forests of east Asia is grown for two main reasons: first, its spreading shape, making it as wide as it is tall; second, its 8in- (20cm-) long, leathery leaves, which are initially bronze-purple before they turn dark green. It produces 1in- (2.5cm-) wide white flowers, but only on mature trees during a long, hot summer with sustained periods at 75°F (24°C) and over. Make sure it is planted in a protected site with adequate shelter from cold, drying winds.

PLANT PROFILE

HEIGHT 40ft (12m)

SPREAD 40ft (12m)

SITE Full sun

SOIL Rich, moist but free-draining

HARDINESS Z7–11 H12–7

E | *Eriobotrya japonica* Loquat

THE EVERGREEN LOQUAT IS a must for anyone with a frost-free,
sheltered garden. It has a superb, open, fingerlike spread of dark
green, leathery, tactile leaves, up to 12in (30cm) long. It will only
flower after a long, hot summer, when it produces clusters of small,
white, scented flowers from late autumn. With a lot of luck they
might be followed in spring by edible, orange-yellow fruits about
1½in (4cm) across. It can also be kept in a large pot and moved into
a conservatory over winter.

PLANT PROFILE

HEIGHT 25ft (8m)

SPREAD 25ft (8m)

SITE Full sun

SOIL Fertile and free-draining

HARDINESS Z8–11 H12–8

Eucalyptus dalrympleana Mountain gum

E

A BEAUTIFUL, UPRIGHT, EVERGREEN TREE, the mountain gum is extremely vigorous, growing at a rate of about 3ft (1m) a year for at least its first 15 years. Later, it slows down by about one-third. The attractive peeling bark is creamy white, while the young leaves are light green (sometimes tinged blue), becoming bright green and leathery, reaching up to 8in (20cm) long. The new, twiggy growth is orange-red. Since most root growth is in the top 12in (30cm) of soil, keep the base free of weeds, which compete for water.

PLANT PROFILE
HEIGHT 70ft (20m)
SPREAD 25ft (8m)
SITE Full sun
SOIL Fertile, preferably neutral to slightly acidic, but tolerates alkalinity
HARDINESS Z9–10 H10–9

E

Eucalyptus gunnii Cider gum

THE EVERGREEN CIDER GUM IS POPULAR for its rounded young leaves, which have a lovely, silvery bluish tinge. The best way to produce an annual show of leaves is to coppice the tree by cutting down the stems to 18in (45cm) above ground in early or midspring. By midsummer the new, spindly growth will be shooting up to 3ft (1m) high or more. Only established trees with a 2in- (5cm-) wide trunk are suitable for coppicing. If they are left to grow naturally, the whitish green bark flakes in late summer, revealing yellowish to grayish green patches. In cold winters, provide a thick mulch. Because this tree is shallow rooting, keep the area around the base free of weeds.

PLANT PROFILE
HEIGHT 30–80ft (10–25m)
SPREAD 20–50ft (6–15m)
SITE Full sun
SOIL Fertile, neutral to slightly acidic
HARDINESS Z8–10 H10–8

Eucryphia x *intermedia* 'Rostrevor'

E

AN UPRIGHT EVERGREEN, 'Rostrevor' is often bushy-headed and has glossy, dark green leaves, providing year-round appeal. The cup-shaped white flowers are about 2in (5cm) wide, and give the garden a boost at the end of summer. The key to growing eucryphias is to provide cool shade at the base of the tree, with the head in plenty of sun. Provide shelter from cold, drying winds unless the area is on the mild side.

PLANT PROFILE
HEIGHT 30ft (10m)
SPREAD 20ft (6m)
SITE Full sun
SOIL Fertile, moist but free-draining, neutral to acidic
HARDINESS Z9–10 H10–9

Eucryphia x *nymansensis*

THE BEST REASONS FOR GROWING this tall, thin, dense evergreen from Chile are its striking, columnar shape (extremely useful in winter) and the late-summer aerial show of clear white flowers, which stand out extremely well against the glossy, dark green leaves. It is slightly fussy and will not tolerate harsh winters, requiring a mild, moist site with shelter in cold areas, especially from chilly, drying winds. Grow where the base of the tree is in the shade and the top gets plenty of sun. Unlike most eucryphias, it will succeed on alkaline soils.

OTHER VARIETY *E.* x *nymansensis* 'Nymansay'.

PLANT PROFILE
HEIGHT 50ft (15m)
SPREAD 15ft (5m)
SITE Full sun
SOIL Fertile, moist but free-draining
HARDINESS Z7–9 H9–8

Euonymus europaeus 'Red Cascade' Spindle tree

E

FORMING A LARGE SHRUB or small tree, the deciduous 'Red Cascade' has a spectacular autumn display of colored leaves and small fruits, which are always best in full sun. The former flare from dark green to red before they fall, while the latter, less than 1in (2.5cm) wide, are also red (*see inset*)—and toxic. They follow the inconspicuous flowers, but you will need two or more plants for a good crop. There are much shorter and taller spindles available, which can be used for everything from ground cover to hedging. 'Red Cascade' thrives on alkaline soil.

OTHER VARIETIES *E. europaeus* 'Aucubifolius';
E. europaeus var. *intermedius.*

PLANT PROFILE	
HEIGHT 10ft (3m)	
SPREAD 8ft (2.5m)	
SITE Full sun or light shade	
SOIL Fertile, free-draining	
HARDINESS Z4–7 H7–1	

E

Euonymus japonicus 'Ovatus Aureus' Japanese spindle

AN EXCELLENT EVERGREEN SPINDLE, this is a cross between a large shrub and a small tree. It is a great favorite due to its variegated leaves, which are dark green with highly distinctive, broad, golden yellow margins. The young spring leaves always have the freshest and best coloring. Make sure it is grown in full sun to achieve first-rate variegation. Provide shelter from cold, drying winds.

OTHER VARIETY *E. japonicus* 'Albomarginatus'.

PLANT PROFILE
HEIGHT 12ft (4m)
SPREAD 6ft (2m)
SITE Full sun or light shade
SOIL Fertile and free-draining
HARDINESS Z6–8 H8–6

Fagus sylvatica European beech

F

THE DECIDUOUS EUROPEAN BEECH is a great sight in spring, when it erupts in shiny green new leaves, and in autumn when the whole canopy flares yellow to orange-brown. The leaf-fall on the ground is equally thrilling. Beech trees are only for very large yards, where they make an impressive sight but rarely live for more than 200 years. There are about 60 different kinds of beech, some with weeping shapes, some with thin outlines, others with a bulging, mushroom canopy or slightly different autumn tones. Seek out a specialist supplier.

OTHER VARIETY *F. sylvatica* 'Dawyck'.

PLANT PROFILE
HEIGHT 80ft (25m)
SPREAD 50ft (15m)
SITE Partial shade
SOIL Free-draining, including alkaline
HARDINESS Z4–7 H9–4

Fagus sylvatica 'Dawyck Purple' Copper beech

A SUPERB BEECH FOR A DOMESTIC SETTING, 'Dawyck Purple' is a very large, narrowly upright tree (*see inset*) with rich, deep, purple foliage. *F. sylvatica* 'Riversii' (*see page 121*) has slightly larger leaves than those of 'Dawyck Purple'. All purple-leaved forms are best grown on a large lawn against an open background to highlight the color and the terrific autumn display, when the leaves turn yellow and then orange-brown. *F. sylvatica* 'Dawyck Gold' makes a good contrast with bright yellow leaves that are green in summer.

PLANT PROFILE

HEIGHT 70ft (20m)

SPREAD 15ft (5m)

SITE Partial shade

SOIL Free-draining, including alkaline

HARDINESS Z5–7 H7–5

Fagus sylvatica var. *heterophylla* 'Aspleniifolia' Fernleaf beech

F

THE FERNLEAF BEECH IS GOOD ENOUGH to be highlighted on an open lawn where it can be fully appreciated, and where it will not be lost among dozens of other trees in a close-planted woodland plan. Also known as the cutleaf beech, it differs from its deciduous parent, *F. sylvatica* (*see page 117*), because it has leaves that range from deeply cut to needlelike. They turn orange-brown in autumn before falling. The midspring flowers appear with the leaves and are followed by husks enclosing nuts. It tolerates a wide range of soils.

PLANT PROFILE
HEIGHT 80ft (25m)
SPREAD 50ft (15m)
SITE Partial shade
SOIL Free-draining, including alkaline
HARDINESS Z5–7 H7–5

OTHER VARIETY *F. sylvatica* var. *heterophylla* f. *laciniata*.

F

Fagus sylvatica 'Pendula' **Weeping beech**

THIS MAKES A GREAT BIG, MOUNDING SHAPE with branches cascading down to the ground and practically touching it, or growing out horizontally with twiggy growth hanging down. When branches do touch the ground, they may take root. Either way, 'Pendula' needs to be isolated on a lawn, where it can be fully appreciated. Any planting behind this tree must take its shadow into account. The spring flowers are followed by husks containing nuts. 'Pendula' makes an extraordinary sight, the complete opposite of 'Dawyck Purple' (*see page 118*), which has a columnar shape.

OTHER VARIETY *F. sylvatica* 'Aurea Pendula'.

PLANT PROFILE
HEIGHT 70–80ft (20–25m)
SPREAD 50ft (15m)
SITE Partial shade
SOIL Free-draining, including alkaline
HARDINESS Z5–7 H7–1

Fagus sylvatica 'Riversii' Purple beech

F

LARGE, DECIDUOUS BEECHES with dark purple leaves come high on some people's plant hate list because they say they just trap the light. Tree expert Alan Mitchell says their ideal place is in a neighbor's garden, a long way off, "with the top just visible." But if you do want one, this is one of several popular cultivars. It must be grown against a bright background to appreciate its color and shape, or both are lost. The flowers are followed by husks containing nuts. 'Riversii' tolerates a wide range of soils. Note that purple-leaved beech trees must be grown in full sun, unlike the yellow-leaved ones, which need partial shade.

OTHER VARIETIES *F. sylvatica* 'Purpurea Pendula'; *F. sylvatica* 'Rohanii'.

PLANT PROFILE	
HEIGHT 80ft (25m)	
SPREAD 50ft (15m)	
SITE Full sun	
SOIL Free-draining, including alkaline	
HARDINESS Z5–7 H7–5	

F *Fagus sylvatica* 'Zlatia' Golden beech

THE BEST REASON FOR GROWING the deciduous golden beech is that the new leaves are a gentle yellow when they unfold in the spring, turning more golden before maturing to green in the summer. It adds a lovely touch to large lawns, and gives a good display again in autumn when the leaves change color and fall. The flowers are followed by husks containing nuts.

OTHER VARIETIES *F. sylvatica* 'Aurea Pendula'; *F. sylvatica* 'Dawyck Gold'.

PLANT PROFILE
HEIGHT 80ft (25m)
SPREAD 50ft (15m)
SITE Full sun
SOIL Free-draining, including alkaline
HARDINESS Z5–7 H7–5

Ficus carica Fruiting fig

F

THE DECIDUOUS FRUITING FIG is an architectural plant with huge, 10in- (25cm-) long leaves, and the edible figs are juicy and sweet. Planted in a backyard, it can grow up to 30ft (10m), but you can reduce it by cramping its root growth. To restrict it to 8ft (2.5m), plant it in a cubical pit, 24in (60cm) on a side, at the foot of a sunny wall. Use paving slabs to line the sides of the pit, and gravel in the base for drainage. Fill with soil. Prune from late spring to midsummer, cutting back young stems to 12in (30cm). Apply tomato fertilizer every two weeks over summer until the fruit ripens.

OTHER VARIETIES   *F. carica* 'Brown Turkey'; *F. carica* 'Brunswick'; *F. carica* 'Goutte d'Or'; *F. carica* 'Rouge de Bourdeaux'; *F. carica* 'Saint Johns'; *F. carica* 'White Marseilles'.

PLANT PROFILE
HEIGHT 8ft (2.5m)
SPREAD 12ft (4m)
SITE Full sun
SOIL Rich, leafy, moist but free-draining
HARDINESS Z7–11 H12–1

F

Fitzroya cupressoides Lahuan

AN IMPRESSIVE, ELEGANT EVERGREEN, this tree comes from Chile and Argentina, where it is now rare, thanks to uncontrolled logging and deforestation. It makes a tall, cylindrical shape and has reddish brown, peeling bark and dark green leaves. The clusters of small flowers (yellow males and yellow-green females) are followed by small brown cones. Provide shelter from cold, drying winds. The genus name commemorates Captain Fitzroy of HMS *Beagle*, on which Charles Darwin sailed on his southern-hemisphere expedition from 1831 to 1836.

PLANT PROFILE

HEIGHT To 50ft (15m)

SPREAD To 20ft (6m)

SITE Full sun

SOIL Average, moist but free-draining

HARDINESS Z7–9 H9–7

Franklinia alatamaha Franklin tree

F

GROWN FOR ITS GLOSSY, DARK GREEN LEAVES, up to 6in (15cm) long, and its camellia-like white flowers, this marvelous deciduous tree used to grow in the wild in the state of Georgia. The flowers are white, showy, and scented, but they appear only after a long, hot summer. They are followed by woody, rounded fruits. The third attraction is the bright red autumn foliage (*see inset*). Provide a sunny, protected site with shelter from cold, drying winds—for example, close to a wall.

PLANT PROFILE
HEIGHT 15ft (5m) or more
SPREAD 15ft (5m)
SITE Full sun
SOIL Rich, moist but free-draining, acidic to neutral
HARDINESS Z6–9 H9–6

F *Fraxinus americana* 'Autumn Purple' White ash

A FAST-GROWING DECIDUOUS ASH, 'Autumn Purple' makes a highly impressive tree. Like its parent, *F. americana*, it has glossy, dark green leaves with a bluish tinge underneath. The male and female flowers appear in clusters on different trees, the latter bearing small winged fruits, or keys. 'Autumn Purple' scores high points because it has particularly good reddish purple color just before the leaves fall; *F. americana* often tends to turn yellow.

OTHER VARIETY *F. americana* 'Rosehill'.

PLANT PROFILE

HEIGHT 60ft (18m)

SPREAD 30ft (10m)

SITE Full sun

SOIL Fertile, moist but free-draining, neutral to alkaline

HARDINESS Z6–9 H9–6

Fraxinus excelsior 'Jaspidea' Golden ash

F

'JASPIDEA' IS A PARTICULARLY ATTRACTIVE FORM of *F. excelsior*, which is tough, quick-growing, and good for coppicing, most trees living for about 200–250 years. What makes 'Jaspidea' a more attractive tree than its parent is its yellow winter shoots (set against black buds), and yellow spring leaves. They turn green in summer, but revert to yellow again in the autumn before falling.

PLANT PROFILE
HEIGHT 70ft (20m)
SPREAD 40ft (12m)
SITE Full sun
SOIL Fertile, moist but free-draining, neutral to alkaline
HARDINESS Z5–8 H8–5

OTHER VARIETIES *F. excelsior* 'Pendula'; *F. excelsior* 'Westhof's Glorie'.

Fraxinus ornus Manna ash

A BUSHY, ROUND–HEADED DECIDUOUS TREE that will not get too big, the manna ash flowers from the end of spring into early summer, when the light scent, like sweet, newly mown hay, attracts plenty of bees. It has a striking show of green-winged seeds, which turn brownish yellow in autumn, and there is also a display of purple-red just before the leaves drop. Like other ashes, it makes an attractive specimen tree, and is perfectly happy in coastal sites. Manna ash also tolerates reasonably dry, acidic to alkaline soils.

OTHER VARIETY *F. ornus* 'Arie Peters'.

PLANT PROFILE

HEIGHT 50ft (15m)

SPREAD 50ft (15m)

SITE Full sun

SOIL Fertile, moist but free-draining

HARDINESS Z6–9 H9–4

Genista aetnensis Mount Etna broom

G

AN EXTREMELY USEFUL, DECIDUOUS, MULTISTEMMED TREE, the Mount Etna broom is quite happy on poor soil, but it must be free-draining. Over winter, its green stems stand out, and then come the spring leaves, after which the tiny, scented, bright yellow flowers appear in mid- to late summer. The whole effect is light and airy, so much so that shorter plants can be grown under its fairly open canopy. *G. aetnensis* needs a sunny, sheltered, protected site bcause it comes from Sardinia and Sicily.

PLANT PROFILE
HEIGHT 25ft (8m)
SPREAD 25ft (8m)
SITE Full sun
SOIL Light, poor to average, free-draining
HARDINESS Z9–11 H12–9

G | *Ginkgo biloba* Maidenhair tree

ANCESTORS OF THE GINKGO DATE BACK to the Jurassic period, about 200 million years ago, while *G. biloba* was grown in Japan 1,000 years ago near temples, making it a good choice for a Japanese-style garden. It also survives modern polluted cities, particularly in the concrete streets beneath skyscrapers. Its distinctive, fan-shaped leaves are about 3in (7.5cm) long and very attractive. The female tree is usually upright with a central stem, while the male tends to be shrubby. The female will not produce edible nuts, encased inside a foul-smelling, fleshy pulp, until it is quite old.

OTHER VARIETIES *G. biloba* 'Autumn Gold'; *G. biloba* 'Fastigiata'; *G. biloba* 'King of Dongting'; *G. biloba* Pendula Group; *G. biloba* 'Saratoga'; *G. biloba* 'Tremonia'.

PLANT PROFILE	
HEIGHT To 100ft (30m)	
SPREAD To 25ft (8m)	
SITE Full sun	
SOIL Fertile, free-draining	
HARDINESS Z5–9 H9–3	

Gleditsia triacanthos 'Rubylace' Honeylocust

G

A TOUGH, VIGOROUS, DECIDUOUS TREE with a fairly open shape, 'Rubylace' has dark bronze-red young leaves that turn bronze-green by midsummer. In autumn, they change again to yellow before they fall. A plus is that in long, hot summers, it may produce large, dangling seed pods. 'Rubylace' is quite happy in dry, dusty city conditions. The only problem is that it is viciously and dangerously spiny, so whatever you do, keep it well away from sidewalks, paths, and children's play areas.

OTHER VARIETIES *G. triacanthos* 'Emerald Cascade'; *G. triacanthos* 'Shademaster'; *G. triacanthos* 'Skyline'.

PLANT PROFILE	
HEIGHT 100ft (30m)	
SPREAD 70ft (20m)	
SITE Full sun	
SOIL Fertile, free-draining	
HARDINESS Z3–7 H7–1	

G | *Gleditsia triacanthos* 'Sunburst' Honeylocust

VERY SIMILAR TO THE DECIDUOUS *Gleditsia triacanthos* 'Rubylace' (*see page 131*), and needing the same conditions, 'Sunburst' has one big advantage: it does not have any thorns, so you can grow it close to where people congregate. Another bonus is that the new, ferny leaves are bright yellow, gradually turning pale green in the summer before returning to yellow in the autumn when they fall. In long, hot summers, it may produce large, dangling seed pods.

OTHER VARIETIES *G. triacanthos* 'Emerald Cascade'; *G. triacanthos* 'Shademaster'; *G. triacanthos* 'Skyline'.

PLANT PROFILE
HEIGHT 40ft (12m)
SPREAD 30ft (10m)
SITE Full sun
SOIL Fertile, free-draining
HARDINESS Z3–7 H7–1

Halesia carolina Silverbell, Snowdrop tree

H

BOTH COMMON NAMES ARE HIGHLY APPROPRIATE because this deciduous, spreading to shrubby tree has small, white, bell-shaped flowers that dangle from thin branches in the spring. The effect is delightful, with the fresh green new leaves quickly following. The flowers later produce small green fruits, which ripen to brown. A further plus comes in autumn, when the leaves turn yellow before falling. Provide shelter from cold, drying winds.

PLANT PROFILE
HEIGHT 25ft (8m)
SPREAD 30ft (10m)
SITE Sun or partial shade
SOIL Fertile, rich, moist but free-draining, neutral to acidic
HARDINESS Z5–8 H8–4

H | *Halesia monticola* Silverbell, Snowdrop tree

THE LATE SPRING FLOWERS of *H. monticola* are larger than those of the very similar *H. carolina* (*see page 133*). They appear either before or at the same time as the leaves, making a delightful show. Another difference is that *H. monticola* is more vigorous, growing into a much larger tree. Provide shelter from cold, drying winds. The related trees *H. monticola* var. *vestita* and var. *vestita* f. *rosea* have larger white flowers and pink–tinged white flowers, respectively.

OTHER VARIETIES *H. monticola* var. *vestita; H. monticola* var. *vestita* f. *rosea.*

PLANT PROFILE
HEIGHT 40ft (12m)
SPREAD 25ft (8m)
SITE Sun or partial shade
SOIL Fertile, rich, moist, and free-draining, neutral to acidic
HARDINESS Z6–9 H9–6

Hoheria 'Glory of Amlwch'

H

THE HIGHPOINT OF 'GLORY OF AMLWCH' comes in summer when there is an excellent display of large, white flowers packed together. This spreading, semievergreen New Zealand tree or large shrub has glossy, bright green leaves up to 4in (10cm) long. In a sunny, sheltered site out of cold winds, it will keep its leaves over winter. The key to success is free-draining soil.

PLANT PROFILE

HEIGHT 22ft (7m)

SPREAD 20ft (6m)

SITE Full sun or partial shade

SOIL Average, moist, and free-draining

HARDINESS Z9–10 H10–9

H | *Hoheria sexstylosa* Ribbonwood

AN EVERGREEN SMALL TREE OR LARGE SHRUB, the ribbonwood has glossy green leaves and, in midsummer, clusters of tiny, pure white flowers. Coming from New Zealand, it needs a sunny, sheltered site away from cold, drying winds. It makes a good specimen plant, and can look very natural with other trees in a woodland garden. The deciduous hoherias, such as *H. glabrata* and *H. lyalii*, are slightly hardier than the evergreens.

OTHER VARIETY *H. sexstylosa* 'Stardust'.

PLANT PROFILE
HEIGHT 25ft (8m)
SPREAD 20ft (6m)
SITE Partial shade
SOIL Average, moist but free-draining
HARDINESS Z9–10 H10–9

Hovenia dulcis Raisin tree

H

THIS IS THE MOST WIDELY GROWN of the two deciduous hovenias. The raisin tree has large, dark green leaves, almost heart-shaped, up to 8in (20cm) long, which are one of its main attractions. The others include the tiny, scented, greenish yellow summer flowers, and the subsequent red, swollen flower stalks, which are fleshy, sweet and edible. They are followed by black fruits. For a good display of flowers, you need a long, hot summer. Provide a sunny, sheltered position where the raisin tree can bask in the heat.

PLANT PROFILE

HEIGHT 40ft (12m)

SPREAD 30ft (10m)

SITE Full sun

SOIL Average, with plenty of humus

HARDINESS Z9–10 H10–9

I | *Idesia polycarpa* Wonder tree

HIGHLY RATED BY THE EXPERTS, but still not as popular as it should be, *I. polycarpa* is grown for two reasons. It has large, almost heart-shaped, dark green leaves, up to 8in (20cm) long, which immediately catch the eye, and clusters of tiny, scented, yellow-green flowers. The most curious thing about the flowers is that they do not have any petals. On female plants they are followed by round, red berries, but you need a long, hot summer for a good crop. In the wild, it grows in the woodlands of China and Japan. A bright, sheltered garden position is important.

PLANT PROFILE

HEIGHT 40ft (12m)

SPREAD 40ft (12m)

SITE Full sun or light shade

SOIL Average, moist but free-draining, tolerates acidity

HARDINESS Z6–9 H9–6

Ilex x *altaclerensis* 'Golden King' Holly

THE BEAUTIFULLY VARIEGATED LEAVES have a gold band around the margin, and are dark green in the middle. The name 'Golden King' is completely misleading because this holly is a female, and to produce any red autumn berries (attracting hungry birds) you need a nearby male, such as the much taller 'Hodginsii'. 'Golden King' is very fast-growing, making an excellent evergreen hedge, but while it tolerates pollution and seaside gardens, it does not like being battered by severe winds. If you are growing it as a hedge, prune it for shape in early spring.

OTHER VARIETY *I.* x *altaclerensis* 'Lawsoniana' (female).

PLANT PROFILE
HEIGHT 20ft (6m)
SPREAD 12ft (4m)
SITE Full sun
SOIL Moist but free-draining, rich in organic matter
HARDINESS Z7–9 H9–7

I

I

Ilex aquifolium 'Argentea Marginata' English holly

A VIGOROUS, VERTICAL COLUMN OF AN EVERGREEN, 'Argentea Marginata' is grown for its leaves (a lovely purple-pink when they unfold), which end up with an attractive, wide, white margin. This tree is a female and, if there is a male nearby, the late spring flowers turn to a lavish show of bright red berries, which are soon eaten by the birds. 'Argentea Marginata' is still sometimes sold as 'Argentea Variegata'. Do not confuse it with the weeping female, 'Argentea Marginata Pendula', which grows only 12ft (4m) high.

OTHER VARIETIES *I. aquifolium* 'Golden Queen' (male); *I. aquifolium* 'Madame Briot' (female); *I. aquifolium* 'Silver Queen' (male).

PLANT PROFILE
HEIGHT To 50ft (15m)
SPREAD 12ft (4m)
SITE Full sun
SOIL Rich, moist but free-draining
HARDINESS Z7–9 H9–7

Ilex aquifolium 'J. C. van Tol' English holly

I

THE GREAT VIRTUE OF 'J. C. VAN TOL' is that it is self-pollinating, which means you do not need an accompanying male to create the show of bright red berries in winter. Growth is much more modest than on some hollies, making it a good choice for a boundary hedge in a medium-sized yard. The leaves are dark green and virtually spineless. Trim hedges for shape if necessary in early spring.

PLANT PROFILE
HEIGHT 20ft (6m)
SPREAD 12ft (4m)
SITE Full sun
SOIL Rich, moist but free-draining
HARDINESS Z7–9 H9–7

OTHER VARIETIES *I. aquifolium* 'Golden Queen' (male); *I. aquifolium* 'Madame Briot' (female); *I. aquifolium* 'Silver Queen' (male).

I

Illicium anisatum Chinese anise

MAKING A SMALL TREE OR LARGE SHRUB, Chinese anise is grown for its small, white, scented flowers, which have open-fingered petals and make an unusual, distinctive sight. The evergreen, glossy, dark green leaves are long and thick, tapering to a point. It is essential that you grow it in a sheltered hot spot, protected from cold, battering winds, and in acidic soil.

PLANT PROFILE
HEIGHT To 25ft (8m)
SPREAD 20ft (6m)
SITE Full sun or partial shade
SOIL Moist but free-draining, humus-rich, acidic
HARDINESS Z7–9 H9–7

Juglans nigra Black walnut

J

A MAGNIFICENT GIANT OF A DECIDUOUS TREE, the black walnut needs to be grown on a huge lawn where it can be admired. Growth is vigorous, with the brown bark turning black in old age. The glossy, dark green leaves, which are divided into leaflets, can be up to 24in (60cm) long, and there is a brief autumn spell when they are yellow, before falling. Each tree has male and female catkins and, when the tree is about ten years old, they produce edible nuts locked inside hard shells within the brown fruits. Plant the black walnut in the right place, because it hates being moved.

OTHER VARIETIES *J. nigra* 'Laciniata'; *J.* 'Paradox'; *J.* 'Red Danube'.

PLANT PROFILE
HEIGHT 100ft (30m)
SPREAD 70ft (20m)
SITE Full sun
SOIL Deep, fertile, free-draining
HARDINESS Z5–9 H9–5

J

Juglans regia Walnut

THE DECIDUOUS WALNUT comes from a large area ranging from China and the Himalayas to central Russia and southeast Europe. It has pale gray bark and leaves that are initially bronze-purple when unfolding in late spring before turning pale brown. The 12in- (30cm-) long leaves consist of seven to nine leaflets, which emit a pungent scent when crushed. Each tree has male and female catkins, eventually followed by edible nuts inside the rounded fruits. Because the catkin flowers may open at slightly different times, another walnut tree nearby ensures a good crop of nuts.

OTHER VARIETIES *J. regia* 'Broadview'; *J. regia* 'Buccaneer'; *J. regia* 'Franquette'; *J. regia* 'Laciniata'; *J. regia* 'Purpurea'.

PLANT PROFILE		
HEIGHT 100ft (30m)		
SPREAD 50ft (15m)		
SITE Full sun		
SOIL Deep, fertile, free-draining		
HARDINESS Z3–7 H7–1		

Juniperus chinensis Chinese juniper

J

AS AN UPRIGHT FORM, the Chinese juniper has plenty of presence and makes a chunky pillar of dark green, scented foliage, but check out plants before buying them, because the shape can vary from tall and columnar to spreading and shrubby. There are several other named forms, providing a range of shapes, heights, and leaf colors, the best including the yellow 'Aurea' and the upright, columnar, misleadingly named 'Pyramidalis'. Coming from the Far East, the Chinese juniper is worth including in Japanese-style gardens, while a young, bushier plant is a good candidate for bonsai.

OTHER VARIETIES *J. chinensis* 'Blaauw'; *J. chinensis* 'Blue Alps'; *J. chinensis* 'Expansa Variegata'; *J. chinensis* 'Kaizuka'; *J. chinensis* 'Variegated Kaizuka'.

PLANT PROFILE
HEIGHT To 70ft (20m)
SPREAD To 20ft (6m)
SITE Full sun or light, dappled shade
SOIL Average, free-draining
HARDINESS Z3–9 H9–1

J

Juniperus communis 'Hibernica' Irish juniper

THIN, UPRIGHT, AND EVERGREEN, the Irish juniper is a bit like a coniferous exclamation mark firing out of the ground; in garden designer's lingo, it is called an accent tree. It is certainly very useful for breaking up the flow of the landscape (making a good contrast against rounded shapes), and guarantees extra winter interest. It is worth a try in formal gardens, especially where it is too cold and windy for *Cupressus sempervirens* (Italian cypress). The flowers (yellow males and green females) are followed by berrylike cones.

OTHER VARIETY *J. communis* 'Sentinel'.

PLANT PROFILE
HEIGHT 10–15ft (3–5m)
SPREAD 12in (30cm)
SITE Full sun or dappled shade
SOIL Free-draining, including dry, alkaline, and sandy soils
HARDINESS Z3–6 H6–1

Juniperus rigida Temple juniper

J

A LARGE, CHUNKY EVERGREEN CONIFER from China and Japan, the temple juniper is a cross between a spreading tree and a large shrub. The brown bark, sometimes with a yellow tinge, is an attractive feature because it peels off. The bright green leaves are like sharply pointed tiny needles, and they turn slightly bronze when the weather gets cold in winter. The flowers (yellow males and green females) are followed by berrylike cones.

OTHER VARIETIES *J. rigida* subsp. *conferta*; *J. rigida* subsp. *conferta* 'Blue Ice'; *J. rigida* subsp. *conferta* 'Blue Pacific'.

PLANT PROFILE
HEIGHT To 25ft (8m)
SPREAD 20ft (6m)
SITE Full sun or dappled shade
SOIL Free-draining, including dry, alkaline, and sandy soils
HARDINESS Z6–9

J

Juniperus squamata 'Chinese Silver' Flaky juniper

THE BEST OF THE CONIFEROUS FLAKY JUNIPERS have eye-catching, gray-blue, needlelike leaves. The large, spreading, shrubby 'Chinese Silver' is silver-blue, as is the 16in- (40cm-) high 'Blue Star', which is best at the front of a border. The much bigger, steely blue 'Meyeri' needs a large, open space where it can spread and arch. Growth gets a bit sloppy, but a regular summer snip keeps 'Chinese Silver' looking neat. The flowers (yellow males and green females) are followed by berrylike cones.

OTHER VARIETY *J. squamata* 'Holger'.

PLANT PROFILE
HEIGHT To 20ft (6m)
SPREAD To 20ft (6m)
SITE Full sun
SOIL Free-draining, including dry, alkaline, and sandy
HARDINESS Z4–9 H9–1

Juniperus virginiana 'Grey Owl' Pencil cedar

AN EXCELLENT, VIGOROUS, GROUND-COVERING JUNIPER, 'Grey Owl' has spreading, horizontal, overlapping branches covered by soft silver-gray leaves, which can be pruned when necessary. The flowers (yellow males and green females) appear on separate plants and are followed by berrylike cones. It can be grown to spread and hang over the edge of a pond, softening the outline and providing a hiding place for frogs. It also contrasts well with deep green, upright junipers like *J. communis* 'Hibernica' (*see page 146*).

OTHER VARIETIES *J. virginiana* 'Blue Cloud'; *J. virginiana* 'Silver Spreader'.

PLANT PROFILE
HEIGHT 6–10ft (2–3m)
SPREAD 10–12ft (3–4m)
SITE Full sun
SOIL Free-draining, including dry, alkaline, and sandy
HARDINESS Z3–9 H9–1

K

Koelreuteria paniculata Golden-rain tree, Pride of India

CLUSTERS OF BRIGHT YELLOW FLOWERS 12in (30cm) long make a lovely sight, but they appear only after a long, hot summer. They are often followed by 2in- (5cm-) long, bladderlike fruits with a pink or red tinge. What you can count on is the pinkish red show of new leaves before they turn green, and their yellow coloring before they fall in autumn. The common name "pride of India" is completely inaccurate—this plant comes from China.

OTHER VARIETIES *K. paniculata* 'Fastigiata'; *K. paniculata* 'Rosseels'.

PLANT PROFILE	
HEIGHT 30ft (10m) or more	
SPREAD 30ft (10m) or more	
SITE Full sun	
SOIL Fertile, free-draining	
HARDINESS Z6–9 H9–1	

+ *Laburnocytisus* 'Adamii'

L

THIS BIZARRE, DECIDUOUS TREE gives no clues for most of the year as to just how extraordinary it suddenly becomes at the end of spring. It has clusters of flowers in three separate colors. The first is bright yellow, the second purple, and the third is purple-pink with a yellow tinge. After that, it goes back into its shell, and is quite ordinary all summer and over winter when it has shed its leaves. For that reason, do not give it too prominent a position, but make sure it can be clearly seen when it is in bloom.

PLANT PROFILE

HEIGHT 25ft (8m)

SPREAD 20ft (6m)

SITE Full sun

SOIL Average, moist but free-draining

HARDINESS Z6–8

L

Laburnum alpinum 'Pendulum' Scotch laburnum

AN EXCELLENT CHOICE FOR SMALL YARDS, this is a modest, slow-growing deciduous tree with all the advantages of much larger laburnums. The stiff, weeping branches carry tumbling clusters of tiny, bright yellow flowers, which stand out nicely against the glossy, dark green leaves. A planting of purple alliums underneath is highly effective. The parent of 'Pendulum' is a much taller, more substantial tree, which can grow 25ft (8m) high. All parts are toxic if eaten.

PLANT PROFILE

HEIGHT 6ft (2m)

SPREAD 6ft (2m)

SITE Full sun

SOIL Average, free-draining

HARDINESS Z5–7

Laburnum x *watereri* 'Vossii' Golden rain

L

THE MOST SENSATIONAL LABURNUM, 'Vossii' makes a tall, deciduous tree dripping in the most lavish way in late spring with long, dangling clusters of tiny yellow flowers. Plant bulbs of *Allium hollandicum* 'Purple Sensation' underneath the boughs to create a superb combination, or, if you have room, make a laburnum tunnel and run groups of 'Purple Sensation' beneath—one of the most magical sights of the gardening year. For the rest of the year, 'Vossii' is quite ordinary, but who cares? Remove any growth at the base of the trunk. All parts are toxic if eaten.

PLANT PROFILE
HEIGHT 25ft (8m)
SPREAD 25ft (8m)
SITE Full sun
SOIL Average, free-draining
HARDINESS Z5–8 H8–3

L | *Lagerstroemia indica* Crepe flower, Crepe myrtle

EITHER A LARGE, DECIDUOUS SHRUB or an upright tree, this
Chinese plant is grown for its 8in- (20cm-) long clusters of white,
pink, or red flowers. It makes a dramatic show over summer, while
in winter the chief attraction is the peeling gray and brown bark.
The crepe flower needs a sunny, sheltered site. If hard pruning is
required, the tree resprouts well.

PLANT PROFILE
HEIGHT 25ft (8m)
SPREAD 25ft (8m)
SITE Full sun
SOIL Average, free-draining
HARDINESS Z7–9 H9–7

OTHER VARIETY *L. indica* 'Rosea'.

Larix decidua European larch

THE HUGE, CONIFEROUS, DECIDUOUS EUROPEAN LARCH quickly shoots up, averaging nearly 2½ft (75cm) per year for the first 20 years. Its branches stick out horizontally, with dangling stems, making it instantly recognizable. Both types of flowers (bright red males and yellow females) appear on the same tree, and are followed by brown cones. Other benefits include the fact that birds love the seeds, and that the leaves turn from green to orange in the autumn before falling.

OTHER VARIETIES *L. decidua* 'Corley'; *L. decidua* 'Globus'; *L. decidua* 'Little Bogle'; *L. decidua* 'Puli'.

PLANT PROFILE	
HEIGHT 100ft (30m)	
SPREAD 12–20ft (4–6m)	
SITE Full sun	
SOIL Deep, free-draining	
HARDINESS Z3–6 H6–1	

L | *Larix kaempferi* Japanese larch

THE CONIFEROUS, DECIDUOUS LARCH from the Far East is easily confused with the European *L. decidua* (*see page 155*), but there are a few key differences. The Japanese larch is a more substantial tree with thicker trunks, its new leaves usually have a bluish tinge, and the twigs have a reddish hue when visible after the leaves have dropped in winter. Both types of flowers (yellow male and creamy to pink female) appear on the same tree in spring, followed by upright cones.

OTHER VARIETIES *L. kaempferi* 'Blue Rabbit Weeping'; *L. kaempferi* 'Diane'; *L. kaempferi* 'Jakobsen's Pyramid'; *L. kaempferi* 'Nana'; *L. kaempferi* 'Pendula'; *L. kaempferi* 'Stiff Weeping'.

PLANT PROFILE

HEIGHT 100ft (30m) or more

SPREAD 12–20ft (4–6m)

SITE Full sun

SOIL Deep, free-draining

HARDINESS Z5–7 H7–4

Laurelia sempervirens

L

SOMETIMES CALLED THE CHILEAN LAUREL, this makes a small evergreen tree or large shrub. To be on the safe side, provide a sheltered position away from cold winds or a space against a sunny wall. The bright green leathery leaves have a marked scent when crushed, and the clusters of tiny, cup-shaped flowers are green. The healthy, glossy foliage makes a good backdrop for other plants.

PLANT PROFILE

HEIGHT 50ft (15m)

SPREAD 30ft (10m)

SITE Full sun or partial shade

SOIL Average, moist but free-draining

HARDINESS Z9–10 H10–9

L

Laurus nobilis 'Aurea' Bay laurel, Sweet bay

IF YOU HAVE COLD, WET, POORLY DRAINED SOIL, evergreen bay must
be grown in a tub filled with free-draining potting mix. Even
gardeners with ideal conditions may plant bay in a container,
clipping it into a short ornamental shape with a long bare stem and
a ball of leaves on top. The latter are used for cooking stews and
soups. Trim for shape in spring and summer. *L. nobilis* has dark green
leaves, and 'Aurea' has golden yellow foliage. Both must be grown in
a sunny, sheltered position away from cold winds; move them into a
greenhouse or other frost-free place in winter.

OTHER VARIETY *L. nobilis* f. *angustifolia*.

PLANT PROFILE
HEIGHT 40ft (12m)
SPREAD 30ft (10m)
SITE Full sun or partial shade
SOIL Moist but free-draining
HARDINESS Z8–10 H12–7

Leptospermum lanigerum Woolly tea tree

L

AN EVERGREEN AUSTRALIAN, the woolly tea tree makes a small tree or large shrub that is grown for its scented, silvery leaves. From late spring there is a good show of cup-shaped white flowers, each about ½in (1cm) wide, with reddish brown in the middle. It needs to be grown in a warm, sheltered site away from cold, drying winds.

PLANT PROFILE
HEIGHT 10–15ft (3–5m)
SPREAD 5–10ft (1.5–3m)
SITE Full sun or partial shade
SOIL Average, free-draining
HARDINESS Z9–10

OTHER VARIETY *L. lanigerum* 'Wellington'.

L | *Ligustrum lucidum* Chinese privet

SOME PEOPLE TURN UP THEIR NOSES at privet, but this evergreen
scores high marks, making a medium-sized tree or large shrub. The
leaves are large, glossy, and dark green, creating an attractive hedge,
large border shrub, or miniature specimen tree. Clusters, up to 8in
(20cm) long, of sweet-scented white flowers are followed by blue-
black fruits in warm regions. It does best in long, hot summers, and
needs shelter from cold winds. Good drainage is important.

OTHER VARIETIES *L. lucidum* 'Excelsum Superbum'; *L. lucidum*
'Golden Wax'; *L. lucidum* 'Tricolor'.

PLANT PROFILE
HEIGHT 30ft (10m)
SPREAD 30ft (10m)
SITE Full sun or partial shade
SOIL Free-draining
HARDINESS Z8–10 H10–8

Liquidambar orientalis Oriental sweetgum

THE DECIDUOUS LIQUIDAMBARS ARE FAMOUS for their sensational autumn color, when the whole tree seems to ignite. The Oriental sweetgum is relatively slow growing and short, and is a good bet for smaller yards. It puts on bushy growth through the summer, and the green leaves turn yellow and orange in the autumn before falling. Give it a prominent position in a sunny, sheltered place.

PLANT PROFILE

HEIGHT 20ft (6m)

SPREAD 12ft (4m)

SITE Full sun

SOIL Average, moist but free-draining, acidic or neutral

HARDINESS Z7–9 H9–7

L | *Liquidambar styraciflua* 'Worplesdon' Sweetgum

'WORPLESDON' HAS DEEPLY CUT LEAVES that turn purple and then orange-yellow in the autumn. The initial dark autumn show means that it needs to be planted against a bright background for the best effect. Given its incredible display, it is worth making sure that it has deep, fertile, moist but free-draining soil. Site it in full sun where the light picks up the colorful autumn leaves, and make sure you can see it clearly. There are several different kinds of *L. styraciflua* with varying features: 'Variegata' has golden yellow markings on the summer leaves; 'Lane Roberts', blackish red leaves in autumn.

OTHER VARIETIES *L. styraciflua; L. styraciflua* 'Burgundy'; *L. styraciflua* 'Golden Treasure'; *L. styraciflua* 'Gum Ball'; *L. styraciflua* 'Lane Roberts'; *L. styraciflua* 'Variegata'.

PLANT PROFILE
HEIGHT 80ft (25m)
SPREAD 40ft (12m)
SITE Full sun
SOIL Average, moist but free-draining, acidic or neutral
HARDINESS Z6–9 H9–6

Liriodendron tulipifera Tulip tree

L

THE COMMON NAME OF TULIP TREE comes from the 2½in- (6cm-) long, pale green, tuliplike flowers (followed by conelike fruits) that appear on the trees, but only when they are 15 to 25 years old. The flowers are not as spectacular as they sound, but still provide an attractive show. The best season is actually autumn, when the leaves turn bright yellow before falling. The winter interest comes from the silver-gray bark, which on mature trees becomes ridged. The tulip tree needs decent soil that does not bake dry for too long.

OTHER VARIETIES *L. tulipifera* 'Aureomarginatum'; *L. tulipifera* 'Fastigiatum'; *L. tulipifera* 'Glen Gold'; *L. tulipifera* 'Mediopictum'.

PLANT PROFILE

HEIGHT 100ft (30m)

SPREAD 50ft (15m)

SITE Full sun or partial shade

SOIL Average, moist but free-draining, slightly acidic

HARDINESS Z5–9 H9–1

L

Luma apiculata Chilean myrtle

MAKING A GIANT EVERGREEN TREE in ideal conditions in its native South America, *L. apiculata* only gets close to that in the mildest coastal regions, and elsewhere makes a large, bushy shrub. It tends to be multistemmed, and the peeling bark is a great attraction, being cinnamon brown and creamy white when exposed. The dark green leaves make a nice contrast, and there are small, cup-shaped white flowers from midsummer, followed by red berries (which end up black) if the summer is long and hot. It needs a sunny, sheltered site.

OTHER VARIETIES *L. apiculata* 'Glanleam Gold'; *L. apiculata* 'Variegata'.

PLANT PROFILE

HEIGHT 30–50ft (10–15m) or more

SPREAD 30–50ft (10–15m) or more

SITE Full sun or partial shade

SOIL Fertile, humus-rich, free-draining

HARDINESS Z9–11 H12–10

Maackia amurensis

M

SLOW-GROWING AND DECIDUOUS, *M. amurensis* makes an open, spreading tree with dark green leaves about 10in (25cm) long, divided into a maximum of 11 leaflets. The tiny flowers appear in small clusters and are followed by flattened seed pods with ridged seams. In the wild, it grows in northeast China. *M. amurensis* is a useful plant if you like something with Far Eastern rarity value.

PLANT PROFILE
HEIGHT To 50ft (15m)
SPREAD To 30ft (10m)
SITE Full sun
SOIL Average, free-draining, neutral to acidic
HARDINESS Z5–7 H7–5

OTHER VARIETY *M. amurensis* var. *buergeri*.

M | *Maclura pomifera* Osage orange

GIVEN AN ADJACENT MALE AND FEMALE OSAGE ORANGE, and a long, hot summer, the females will produce large, wrinkled, yellow–green, inedible fruits. They can be up to 5in (12cm) wide, and have seeds within a fleshy pulp. The fruits also help to make *M. pomifera* an attractive hedge, but do not plant it where children play because it has sharp, vicious spines. Osage orange is not fussy and thrives without any pampering.

PLANT PROFILE

HEIGHT 50ft (15m)

SPREAD 40ft (12m)

SITE Full sun

SOIL Average, free-draining

HARDINESS Z5–9 H9–5

Magnolia campbellii

M

LARGE AND DECIDUOUS, *M. campbellii* is one of the finest magnolias because its 16-petaled flowers (white or crimson to rose pink) can be absolutely enormous, up to 12in (30cm) wide. Plant collector Frank Kingdon Ward saw them in the wild in India, saying their "blooms toss like white horses." Trees can be multistemmed, with leaves up to 10in (25cm) long. Avoid buying one grown from seed, which can take 25 years to flower; otherwise, expect a wait of up to ten years. A mild, frost-free, sheltered site is vital or the flowers will get damaged. Mulch to stop the soil from drying out over summer.

OTHER VARIETIES *M. campbellii* Alba Group; *M. campbellii* 'Darjeeling'; *M. campbellii* subsp. *mollicomata*; *M. campbellii* 'Charles Raffill' (Raffill Group).

PLANT PROFILE
HEIGHT 50ft (15m)
SPREAD 30ft (10m)
SITE Sun or partial shade
SOIL Moist but free-draining, humus-rich, acidic to neutral
HARDINESS Z7–9 H9–7

M | *Magnolia* 'Heaven Scent'

AN EXCELLENT DECIDUOUS MAGNOLIA for a medium-sized yard, 'Heaven Scent' makes an upright tree. It is incredibly popular because it always gives a good display of strongly scented flowers, the petals packed together like those of a tulip (*see inset*) before gradually opening up. Because it flowers in midspring, it ideally needs a sunny, sheltered site where the scent can hang in the air. On an open lawn slashed by strong winds, the scent can get blasted away. Mulch to prevent the soil from drying out over the summer. Avoid seed-raised plants, since they take much longer to come into flower for the first time.

PLANT PROFILE

HEIGHT 30ft (10m)

SPREAD 30ft (10m)

SITE Sun or partial shade

SOIL Moist but free-draining, humus-rich, acidic

HARDINESS Z6–9 H9–6

Magnolia kobus

M

HARDY AND DECIDUOUS, *M. kobus* has 8in- (20cm-) long leaves, with a strong scent when crushed, and white flowers up to 4in (10cm) wide. It is beautiful when covered in blooms, but note two potential problems. Flowers do not appear on young plants (you might have to wait until the tree is ten years old, or much longer if it has been raised from seed), and they can be ruined by frost. For that reason, plant *M. kobus* in a sunny, sheltered site. Apply a mulch around the base to stop the soil from drying out over the summer.

OTHER VARIETY *M. kobus* var. *borealis*.

PLANT PROFILE
HEIGHT 40ft (12m)
SPREAD 30ft (10m)
SITE Sun or partial shade
SOIL Moist but free-draining, humus-rich, acidic to neutral
HARDINESS Z5–9 H9–5

M | *Magnolia* x *loebneri* 'Merrill'

HIGHLY VALUED FOR ITS PURE WHITE, slightly scented flowers, 'Merrill' grows a vertical, vigorous 30ft (10m) high. The flowers are initially goblet-shaped but end up looking more like stars, each one with 15 broad, white petals. They appear before the leaves. Provide a sheltered site and mulch generously to prevent the soil from drying out over summer. Avoid seed-raised plants, since they take a long time to come into flower.

OTHER VARIETIES *M.* x *loebneri* 'Ballerina'; *M.* x *loebneri* 'Leonard Messel'.

PLANT PROFILE
HEIGHT 30ft (10m)
SPREAD 25ft (8m)
SITE Sun or partial shade
SOIL Moist but free-draining, humus-rich, acidic to neutral
HARDINESS Z5–9 H9–1

Magnolia salicifolia 'Wada's Memory' Willowleaf magnolia   M

A GOOD CHOICE FOR A MEDIUM-SIZED YARD—though in one case, a 40-year-old specimen has actually reached 40ft (12m) high—'Wada's Memory' has slightly scented flowers in midspring. Although the flowers (which appear on young plants) do not stay at their best for very long, the petals hang on and look lovely when ruffled by the wind. The new leaves unfold mahogany red after the flowers open on bare branches; the leaves then turn green as they mature. Plant in a sheltered site, and mulch to prevent the soil from drying out over summer. Avoid seed-raised plants.

PLANT PROFILE

HEIGHT 28ft (9m)

SPREAD 22ft (7m)

SITE Sun or partial shade

SOIL Moist but free-draining, humus-rich, acidic to neutral

HARDINESS Z6–9 H9–6

M | *Magnolia wilsonii*

NAMED AFTER PLANT HUNTER ERNEST WILSON (1876–1930), this magnolia makes a small deciduous tree or a large, spreading, multistemmed shrub with leathery, bright green leaves up to 8in (20cm) long. The highly scented flowers are great beauties, like white cups with a dash of red in the center, producing a stunning show in spring. Provide a sheltered site to make sure they are not damaged by frost. New trees should start to flower when they are five years old; seed-raised plants take much longer. Prevent the soil from drying out over the summer by applying a mulch around the base.

OTHER VARIETY *M. wilsonii* 'Gwen Baker'.

PLANT PROFILE
HEIGHT 20ft (6m)
SPREAD 20ft (6m)
SITE Sun or partial shade
SOIL Moist but free-draining, humus-rich, acidic to neutral
HARDINESS Z7–9 H9–7

Malus 'Butterball' Crabapple

M

SMALL AND SPREADING, this crabapple is a decent deciduous choice for a medium-sized yard. It has two seasons of interest: in the spring, after the gray-green leaves have appeared (later turning green), it is covered in white flowers with a pink tinge; these are later followed by a striking show of orange-yellow fruits, which initially have a red flush. The fruits attract birds; they are edible and nutritious, and good for making crabapple jelly. Like all the crabapples, 'Butterball' is easy to grow, but avoid over-rich soils and provide a sunny position for the best show.

OTHER VARIETIES *M.* 'Evereste'; *M.* 'Winter Gold'.

PLANT PROFILE
HEIGHT 25ft (8m)
SPREAD 25ft (8m)
SITE Full sun
SOIL Average, moist but free-draining
HARDINESS Z5–8

M *Malus floribunda* Japanese crabapple

A MASS OF RED BUDS produces a profusion of pale pink flowers in mid- and late spring, making the Japanese crabapple a good choice for medium-sized yards. The flowers are followed by tiny yellow fruits, and these attract birds. This deciduous tree has dense growth and graceful, arching branches. Straightforward to grow, the Japanese crabapple is best in full sun and does not like soil that is too rich.

PLANT PROFILE
HEIGHT 30ft (10m)
SPREAD 30ft (10m)
SITE Full sun
SOIL Average, moist but free-draining
HARDINESS Z4–8 H8–1

Malus hupehensis Crabapple

M

A DECIDUOUS CHINESE TREE, *M. hupehensis* puts on a big show at the end of spring, when it produces a foaming mass of scented white flowers. They are followed by a highly impressive display of tiny red fruits, which attract birds. There is an extra autumn bonus when the leaves color up before falling. And in winter the orange-brown bark is clearly visible after leaf-fall. As with other crabapples, give it a sunny spot and avoid over-rich soils. The plant hunter Ernest Wilson said that *M. hupehensis* was one of the best flowering trees he brought back from China.

PLANT PROFILE
HEIGHT 40ft (12m)
SPREAD 40ft (12m)
SITE Full sun
SOIL Average, moist but free-draining
HARDINESS Z5–8 H8–5

M

Malus 'John Downie' Crabapple

'JOHN DOWNIE' HAS A BIG REPUTATION for its abundance of top-quality orange and red fruits. They entice birds, and are edible and nutritious when cooked, being mainly used to make crabapple jelly. The spring show begins with the pale pink buds, which are followed by white flowers. The deciduous growth is upright when young, becoming conical with age. 'John Downie' is good for medium-sized yards, where it tolerates some shade. Avoid planting it in recently fertilized soil.

OTHER VARIETIES *M.* 'Marshal Ôyama'; *M.* 'Red Jade'.

PLANT PROFILE
HEIGHT 30ft (10m)
SPREAD 20ft (6m)
SITE Full sun
SOIL Average, moist but free-draining
HARDINESS Z4–8 H8–1

Malus x *moerlandsii* 'Profusion' Crabapple

M

IF YOU NEED A CONTRAST to a white-flowering crabapple, go for 'Profusion', because it is noted for its terrific show of faintly scented, dark purple-pink flowers in late spring. That color scheme is backed up by purple-red young leaves, which turn bronze-green. Later, the flowers are followed by small, reddish purple fruits.

OTHER VARIETIES *M.* x *gloriosa* 'Oekonomierat Echtermeyer'; *M.* x *moerlandsii* 'Liset'; *M.* x *purpurea* 'Aldenhamensis'; *M.* x *purpurea* 'Eleyi'; *M.* x *purpurea* 'Lemoinei'.

PLANT PROFILE
HEIGHT 30ft (10m)
SPREAD 30ft (10m)
SITE Full sun
SOIL Average, moist but free-draining
HARDINESS Z4–8 H8–1

M | *Malus* x *robusta* 'Red Sentinel' Crabapple

THE BIG SHOW, ONE OF THE BEST AMONG CRABAPPLES, comes in autumn with the long-lasting, dark red fruits. They hang on for much of the winter, attracting birds, and are delicious when cooked, usually for making into crabapple jelly. 'Red Sentinel' is deciduous and makes a very good choice for small- or medium-sized yards, compensating for its relatively modest stature in the spring with a multitude of white flowers. Site it in full sun, avoiding rich soils.

OTHER VARIETIES *M.* x *robusta* 'Red Siberian'; *M.* x *robusta* 'Yellow Siberian'.

PLANT PROFILE
HEIGHT 22ft (7m)
SPREAD 22ft (7m)
SITE Full sun
SOIL Average, moist but free-draining
HARDINESS Z4–8 H8–1

Malus 'Royalty' Crabapple

M

PURPLE IS THE DOMINANT COLOR of 'Royalty'. The new leaves are dark purple when they emerge in the spring, though they turn paler through the summer, before reddening up in preparation for the autumn leaf-fall. And the mid- and late spring flowers are crimson-purple. The color theme is repeated in the autumn with the dark red fruits. They are irresistible to birds, and make a tasty crabapple jelly. For the best flowers and fruits on this spreading tree, choose a sunny position in soil that is not too fertile.

OTHER VARIETIES   *M. x gloriosa* 'Oekonomierat Echtermeyer'; *M. x moerlandsii* 'Liset'; *M. x purpurea* 'Aldenhamensis'; *M. x purpurea* 'Eleyi'; *M. x purpurea* 'Lemoinei'.

PLANT PROFILE
HEIGHT 25ft (8m)
SPREAD 25ft (8m)
SITE Full sun
SOIL Average, moist but free-draining
HARDINESS Z5–8 H8–5

M | *Malus* x *scheideckeri* 'Red Jade' Crabapple

'RED JADE' HAS ATTRACTIVE, WEEPING GROWTH, giving it a much greater width than height. Its deciduous growth sometimes has a shrubby appearance. In late spring it is covered in red buds and then white flowers (possibly with a pink tinge); they are followed by glossy, bright red fruits. If you can harvest the fruits before the birds, they make a good crabapple jelly. Sunny conditions and moderately fertile soils produce the best results.

OTHER VARIETY *M.* 'Royal Beauty'.

PLANT PROFILE

HEIGHT 12ft (4m)

SPREAD 20ft (6m)

SITE Full sun

SOIL Average, moist but free-draining

HARDINESS Z4–8 H6–1

Malus tschonoskii Crabapple

M

IT IS SOMETIMES KNOWN AS THE PILLAR TREE because its growth is smartly upright. The spring flowers give a show of white with a pink tinge, and are followed by yellow-green fruits that attract birds and are delicious and nutritious when cooked. The autumn flare-up is among the best of the crabapples because the leaves turn brilliant yellow-orange, red, and purple before falling. Another advantage of *M. tschonoskii* is that it tolerates quite poor soils.

PLANT PROFILE

HEIGHT 40ft (12m)

SPREAD 22ft (7m)

SITE Full sun

SOIL Average, moist but free-draining

HARDINESS Z5–8 H8–5

M

Malus x *zumi* var. *calocarpa* 'Golden Hornet' Crabapple

HIGHLY RATED SINCE ITS INTRODUCTION IN 1949, 'Golden Hornet' has shapely, deciduous growth and an excellent display of bright yellow fruits that hang on for quite a long time. The fruits are a magnet for birds, and make excellent crabapple jelly. The preceding spring flowers are white with a pink flush. The autumn leaf show is well worth waiting for because the foliage turns from green to gold and then reddish purple. Plenty of sun, and soil not overloaded with nutrients produce the best fruits.

OTHER VARIETIES *M.* 'Evereste'; *M.* 'Winter Gold'.

PLANT PROFILE
HEIGHT 30ft (10m)
SPREAD 25ft (8m)
SITE Full sun
SOIL Average, moist but free-draining
HARDINESS Z4–8 H8–1

Maytenus boaria Maiten

M

THIS DROOPING, WEEPING CHILEAN EVERGREEN deserves to be much more widely grown. In the average backyard it makes either a large shrub or a modest tree, growing to about 35ft (11m) high and 15ft (5m) wide. The small foliage catches the eye in the spring, when there is a nice mix of the old dark green leaves and the new ones, which start out pale green. At the same time there are tiny, pale green flowers sometimes followed by small red fruits. Maiten is unlikely to survive cold, wet, winters, especially if there is bad drainage.

OTHER VARIETY *M. boaria* 'Worplesdon Fastigiate'.

PLANT PROFILE

HEIGHT 70ft (20m)

SPREAD To 30ft (10m)

SITE Full sun

SOIL Average, moist but free-draining

HARDINESS Z9–10

M | *Mespilus germanica* Medlar

THE VICTORIANS LOVED THE FLESHY, BROWN, APPLELIKE FRUIT of the medlar (fermented and sweetened), but when raw it is quite inedible. Most people now use it for making jelly. The deciduous tree is worth growing, making a spreading shape that needs to be highlighted on an open lawn and not hidden away. There are white flowers (sometimes pink-tinged) in late spring and, with luck, good autumn color when the leaves turn yellow-brown before falling.

OTHER VARIETIES *M. germanica* 'Dutch'; *M. germanica* 'Large Russian'; *M. germanica* 'Nottingham'.

PLANT PROFILE
HEIGHT 20ft (6m)
SPREAD 25ft (8m)
SITE Full sun
SOIL Average, moist but free-draining
HARDINESS Z6–9 H9–6

Metasequoia glyptostroboides Dawn redwood

M

THE ULTIMATE IN VERTICAL GIANTS, this deciduous conifer is amazingly impressive, but you can only grow it if you have a huge yard. The outer bark is soft, spongy, and orange-brown. Bright green leaves appear early in the spring and do not drop until late autumn. In the 1940s, the dawn redwood was rediscovered growing wild in China, and was then widely planted in arboretums around the world. It is a quick grower, especially when summers are hot and rainfall is regular.

OTHER VARIETIES *M. glyptostroboides* 'Gold Rush'; *M. glyptostroboides* 'Sheridan Spire'.

PLANT PROFILE
HEIGHT 100ft (30m)
SPREAD 15ft (5m)
SITE Full sun
SOIL Humus-rich, moist but free-draining
HARDINESS Z4–11 H12–1

M | *Morus alba* White mulberry

THE WHITE MULBERRY IS BEST KNOWN for providing the leaves eaten by silkworms. Like other mulberry trees, it can live for hundreds of years and puts on slow, spreading, deciduous growth with mature, gnarled bark, creating a lovely sight in a large lawn. The large, glossy, bright green leaves turn yellow before they fall. The autumn also sees the white fruits ripening to tastier pink and red (*see inset*). All mulberries are self-fertile, with male and female flowers on the same tree. The white mulberry is not as tough as the black (*M. nigra, see opposite*), which is a better bet in cold regions. Provide a sheltered position.

OTHER VARIETIES *M. alba* 'Laciniata'; *M. alba* 'Pendula'; *M. alba* 'Platanifolia'.

PLANT PROFILE
HEIGHT 30ft (10m)
SPREAD 30ft (10m)
SITE Full sun
SOIL Average, moist but free-draining
HARDINESS Z4–8 H8–1

Morus nigra Black mulberry

M

THIS DECIDUOUS TREE is slightly more rounded than the similar *M. alba* (*see opposite*), and the leaves are consistently heart-shaped. They are also dark green, and turn yellow before they fall in autumn. The fruit is tastier than the white mulberry, and can be eaten fresh or in preserves. Let the fruit ripen before picking, and do not bruise it (trees are best grown in lawns because this provides a soft landing). As the fruit is ripening, water the tree well if the ground is baking dry. Provide shelter from cold winds.

OTHER VARIETIES *M. nigra* 'Chelsea'; *M. nigra* 'Large Black'.

PLANT PROFILE
HEIGHT 40ft (12m)
SPREAD 50ft (15m)
SITE Full sun
SOIL Average, moist but free-draining
HARDINESS Z5–9 H9–5

N | *Nothofagus antarctica* Antarctic beech

MODERATE COLD WILL NOT BE A PROBLEM for this deciduous, often multistemmed tree or shrub from southern South America. The tree's shape tends to be attractively irregular (*see inset*), with open growth high up, particularly evident when it is bare of leaves in winter. Glossy, dark green leaves start unfolding in the spring, and are crinkled or wavy at the margins. They turn yellow in the autumn before falling. The Antarctic beech is usually grown in woodlands or large gardens. Its flowers and fruits are insignificant.

PLANT PROFILE	
HEIGHT 50ft (15m)	
SPREAD 30ft (10m)	
SITE Full sun	
SOIL Fertile, moist but free-draining, acidic	
HARDINESS Z7–10 H10–7	

Nothofagus dombeyi Southern beech

N

THE DARK GREEN, EVERGREEN LEAVES (with finely serrated edges) are surprisingly small on such a large tree, giving it a relatively open, delicate, completely unoppressive look. The bark is an added attraction on older trees because it turns from dark gray to reddish brown. The insignificant flowers appear in late spring, and are followed by bristly husks with three small nuts inside.

PLANT PROFILE
HEIGHT 70ft (20m)
SPREAD 30ft (10m)
SITE Full sun
SOIL Fertile, moist but free-draining, acidic
HARDINESS Z8–9 H9–8

N | *Nyssa sinensis* Chinese tupelo

THE AUTUMN SHOW of the deciduous, sometimes multistemmed Chinese tupelo is its great asset. The young bronze leaves, about 8in (20cm) long, turn dark green in the summer, and then brilliant shades of orange, red, and yellow before falling, making a bright, flamboyant sight. Growing it by a large pond doubles the effect, with the colorful reflection in the water. The flowers are tiny and inconspicuous. Provide shelter from cold, drying winds.

OTHER VARIETY *N. sinensis* Nymans form.

PLANT PROFILE

HEIGHT 30ft (10m)

SPREAD 30ft (10m)

SITE Sun or partial shade

SOIL Fertile, moist but free-draining, neutral to acidic

HARDINESS Z7–9 H9–7

Nyssa sylvatica Black gum, Sour gum, Tupelo

N

THE BEST REASON FOR GROWING THE BLACK GUM is the sensational show of autumn color. As the green chlorophyll fades in the foliage, flashy orange, yellow, and red pigments leap to the forefront (in most years, you get the full sweep of color; in bad years the show is more muted). Acidic soil and full sun generally produce the best leaf color.

OTHER VARIETIES *N. sylvatica* 'Autumn Cascades'; *N. sylvatica* 'Jermyns Flame'; *N. sylvatica* 'Sheffield Park'; *N. sylvatica* 'Windsor'; *N. sylvatica* 'Wisley Bonfire'.

PLANT PROFILE	
HEIGHT 70ft (20m)	
SPREAD 30ft (10m)	
SITE Sun or partial shade	
SOIL Fertile, moist but free-draining, neutral to acidic	
HARDINESS Z4–9 H9–2	

O | *Ostrya virginiana* Americam hop hornbeam, Ironwood

TOLERATING A WIDE RANGE OF SOILS, the deciduous *O. virginiana* makes a rounded or conical shape. It is not widely available, but you should be able to track one down. The dark green leaves turn warm yellow in autumn before falling. The 2in- (5cm-) long catkins bring the branches to life in the spring, and are followed by creamy white husks (*see inset*), which ripen to brown in autumn, enclosing a nut.

PLANT PROFILE	
HEIGHT 50ft (15m)	
SPREAD 40ft (12m)	
SITE Sun or partial shade	
SOIL Fertile, free-draining	
HARDINESS Z5–9 H9–2	

Oxydendrum arboreum Sorrel tree, Sourwood

O

A SMALL, SLOW-GROWING DECIDUOUS TREE or large shrub, the sorrel tree is grown for its flashy autumn colors. The 8in- (20cm-) long, glossy, dark green leaves (grayish green beneath) turn fantastic shades of bright red, yellow, and purple before falling if given full sun. Before then, in late summer and early autumn, it produces sprays and clusters of lovely tubular or urn-shaped white flowers, followed by whitish fruits. Note that moist, acidic soil is important.

PLANT PROFILE
HEIGHT 30–50ft (10–15m)
SPREAD 25ft (8m)
SITE Full sun
SOIL Fertile, moist but free-draining, acidic
HARDINESS Z5–9 H9–3

P

Parrotia persica Persian ironwood

THE PERSIAN IRONWOOD MAKES A SMALL, SPREADING TREE or large, deciduous bushy shrub. Either way, it is one of the first to launch into its autumn leaf show of yellow, followed by orange and reddish purple, and the performance is definitely top-notch. A few months later, toward the end of winter, clusters of tiny, spiderlike red flowers appear before the leaves. A third attraction is the peeling bark, with pieces of gray flaking off to reveal pink and cream marbling.

OTHER VARIETIES   *P. persica* 'Burgundy'; *P. persica* 'Lamplighter'; *P. persica* 'Pendula'; *P. persica* 'Vanessa'.

PLANT PROFILE
HEIGHT 25ft (8m)
SPREAD 30ft (10m)
SITE Full sun or partial shade
SOIL Fertile, moist but free-draining
HARDINESS Z4–7 H7–1

Paulownia tomentosa Empress tree, Foxglove tree

P

THERE ARE TWO WAYS OF GROWING THE FOXGLOVE TREE. If you leave it as nature intended, it will make a fast-growing tree with large, bright green leaves up to 12in (30cm) long, and an abundant show of late spring flowers, which are pinkish lilac with purple and yellow marks inside. Alternatively, cut it back to the ground in the spring, allowing one strong, vigorous shoot to fire straight up like a flagpole (cut off the weaker ones). This shoot will produce a few massive leaves up to 2ft (60cm) long. Make it the central point of a small planting, surrounded by bright, subtropical plants. Provide a warm, sheltered site.

OTHER VARIETY *P. tomentosa* 'Coreana'.

PLANT PROFILE
HEIGHT 40ft (12m)
SPREAD 30ft (10m)
SITE Full sun
SOIL Fertile, free-draining
HARDINESS Z5–8 H8–5

P *Phellodendron amurense* Amur cork tree

THE "CORK" PART OF THE COMMON NAME refers to the soft, thick, corky bark that develops on mature trees. Amur cork trees have a spreading shape and, given long hot summers, shoot up quite quickly. The leaves consist of up to 13 glossy, dark green leaflets, which turn yellow in autumn. Because male and female flowers are borne on separate trees, one of each is needed to produce fruits. While the green flowers are on the small side, the males do have yellow in the center, which stands out in midsummer. On female trees, flowers are followed by green fruits that ripen to black. Note that new growth can be stunted by spring frosts.

OTHER VARIETY *P. amurense* var. *sachalinense.*

PLANT PROFILE	
HEIGHT 46ft (14m)	
SPREAD 50ft (15m)	
SITE Full sun	
SOIL Fertile, free-draining	
HARDINESS Z4–7 H8–5	

Phillyrea latifolia Mock privet

MAKING A SMALL, DENSE, ROUNDED EVERGREEN TREE, large shrub, or even a hedge, *P. latifolia*'s chief asset is its mass of small, glossy, dark green leaves. The little flowers are an inconspicuous greenish white, while the round, blue–black fruits rarely develop in the average backyard. Provide shelter from cold, drying winds. In areas prone to frost, grow it against a sunny, protective wall. Good drainage is very important for a healthy tree.

PLANT PROFILE

HEIGHT	To 28ft (9m)
SPREAD	To 28ft (9m)
SITE	Full sun
SOIL	Fertile, free-draining
HARDINESS	Z7–9 H9–7

P | *Picea abies* Norway spruce

BEST KNOWN AS THE TRADITIONAL CHRISTMAS TREE, *P. abies* is an evergreen conifer that makes an impressive landscape plant. The shape is initially conical but gradually becomes more columnar, with dark green winter leaves and long brown cones.

PLANT PROFILE

HEIGHT 70–130ft (20–40m)

SPREAD 20ft (6m)

SITE Full sun

SOIL Moist but free-draining, neutral to acidic

HARDINESS Z3–8 H8–1

OTHER VARIETIES *P. abies* 'Acrocona'; *P. abies* 'Ohlendorffii'.

Picea breweriana Brewer spruce

P

EVENTUALLY MAKING A LARGE, CHUNKY, DRAMATIC TREE, the evergreen, coniferous Brewer spruce is slow-growing—irritatingly so for the first ten years. Its shape is a bit like a baggy pyramid, with the side branches sticking out horizontally. It has small, dark green leaves, and the tiny, needlelike flowers (red males and red or green females) are followed by 4½in- (12cm-) long, reddish brown cones. It is important to provide moist soil that never bakes dry.

PLANT PROFILE
HEIGHT 30–50ft (10–15m)
SPREAD 10–12ft (3–4m)
SITE Full sun
SOIL Moist but free-draining, neutral to acidic
HARDINESS Z6–8 H8–6

P

Picea glauca var. *albertiana* 'Conica' White spruce

THIS EVERGREEN, CONIFEROUS, BUSHY SPRUCE often hits only 15ft (5m) and takes about 20 years to get there. The shape is like a wobbly pyramid or cone, densely covered with needlelike leaves; the new spring leaves are fresh, light green. The flowers (red males and purple-red females) appear in the spring, the latter being followed by 2in- (5cm-) long, light brown cones. 'Conica' is prone to attack by red spider mites in long hot spells; a regular spray treatment tackles the problem.

PLANT PROFILE

HEIGHT 6–20ft (2–6m)

SPREAD 3–8ft (1–2.5m)

SITE Full sun

SOIL Moist but free-draining, neutral to acidic

HARDINESS Z2–6 H6–1

Picea omorika Serbian spruce

P

AN EVERGREEN, SPIRELIKE CONIFER, the Serbian spruce puts on quick, vertical growth, slightly bushier at the bottom than the top, where the peak is slender. The short branches tend to arch down, but point up at the tips. It must be planted with care because of the shade it will cast. The Serbian spruce is remarkably tolerant of poor conditions. The tiny, red spring flowers are followed by egg-shaped, purple-brown cones.

PLANT PROFILE
HEIGHT 70ft (20m)
SPREAD 6–10ft (2–3m)
SITE Full sun
SOIL Moist but free-draining, neutral to acidic
HARDINESS Z4–8 H8–1

OTHER VARIETY *P. omorika* 'Nana'.

P

Picea orientalis 'Skylands' Caucasian spruce, Oriental spruce

WITH BRIGHT GOLDEN YELLOW LEAVES, this coniferous evergreen needs a background of dark green leaves so that the color really stands out. When the male flowers are yellow, they are hard to see against the yellow foliage, but when they turn red they put on an excellent show, as do the 4in- (10cm-) long, purple-brown cones. Growth is initially conical and slow, but soon picks up. Provide protection from cold winds.

OTHER VARIETIES *P. orientalis*; *P. orientalis* 'Aurea'.

PLANT PROFILE
HEIGHT 100ft (30m)
SPREAD 20–25ft (6–8m)
SITE Full sun
SOIL Moist but free-draining, neutral to acidic
HARDINESS Z5–8 H8–5

Picea pungens 'Hoopsii' Colorado spruce

P

A STARTLING SILVER–BLUE, 'Hoopsii' makes an irregular, evergreen pyramid with a central growing point and horizontal branches that are longer lower down. The dense, needlelike leaves are quite pointed and long and, from a distance, look a bit like clusters of sausages. With summer pruning, you can keep this spruce pyramidal and relatively short. The spring flowers (reddish males and green females) are followed by 4in- (10cm-) long pale brown cones. Make sure the tree has bright sun.

OTHER VARIETIES *P. pungens* 'Erich Frahm'; *P. pungens* 'Globosa'; *P. pungens* 'Iseli Fastigiate'; *P. pungens* 'Koster'; *P. pungens* 'Thuem'.

PLANT PROFILE
HEIGHT 50ft (15m)
SPREAD To 15ft (5m)
SITE Full sun
SOIL Moist but free-draining, neutral to acidic
HARDINESS Z3–8 H8–1

P

Picea smithiana Morinda spruce

A HIGHLY RATED SPRUCE found from Afghanistan to western Nepal, the Morinda spruce develops a central, vertical stem that shoots up and up, with horizontal branches sticking out and mini-branches dangling down. There are evergreen, dark green leaves, tiny flowers from late spring to early summer, and brown cones (initially green), which are about 6in (15cm) long. *P. smithiana* needs a large yard and plenty of space so that you can stand back and admire it. It is also a good see-through choice if you want to avoid the dense, solid, chunky spruces that block all views behind them.

PLANT PROFILE
HEIGHT 70–100ft (20–30m)
SPREAD 20–28ft (6–9m)
SITE Full sun
SOIL Moist but free-draining, neutral to acidic
HARDINESS Z7–8 H8–1

Picrasma quassioides Quassia

P

THE FAR EASTERN, DECIDUOUS QUASSIA has excellent autumn colors. The leaves consist of 9 to 15 glossy green leaflets that first turn yellow, then orange and red in the autumn before they fall. An extra attraction is the green spring flowers, which are tiny and bowl-like, and appear in clusters up to 6in (15cm) long. It grows best in acidic soils, and is usually placed at the edge of a woodland setting.

PLANT PROFILE
HEIGHT 25ft (8m)
SPREAD 25ft (8m)
SITE Full sun or partial shade
SOIL Fertile, free-draining
HARDINESS Z6–9 H9–6

P | *Pinus aristata* Bristlecone pine

A SMALL, EVERGREEN, CONIFEROUS TREE OR LARGE SHRUB, the
bristlecone pine makes a dense, conical tree and is a tough
survivor—some wild North American specimens are thought to be
about 2,000 years old. The branches, which turn up at the tips, are
covered in bright green, needlelike leaves with flecks of white.
When the new needles appear on young stems, they have a hint of
blue-white on the inward-facing side. The leaves then last about 20
years. The tiny flowers are followed by brown cones, up to 4in
(10cm) long. Avoid shade and polluted areas.

OTHER VARIETIES *P. aristata* 'Cecilia'; *P. aristata* 'Sherwood
Compact'.

PLANT PROFILE	
HEIGHT 30ft (10m)	
SPREAD 20ft (6m)	
SITE Full sun	
SOIL Average, free-draining	
HARDINESS Z2–10 H9–1	

Pinus bungeana Lacebark pine

P

A NICE MIX OF YELLOW-GREEN, NEEDLELIKE LEAVES and attractive, colorful bark distinguishes this slow-growing, evergreen, coniferous tree. The bark is gray-green but has a mottled look because small scales keep peeling off; the exposed color underneath can be anything from yellow to purple-red. The tiny flowers (purple males and red females) are followed by yellow-brown cones up to 3in (7cm) long. The lacebark pine was discovered in China in 1831 and is now widely available. It does not thrive in shade or polluted areas.

OTHER VARIETY *P. bungeana* 'Diamant'.

PLANT PROFILE
HEIGHT 30–50ft (10–15m)
SPREAD 15–20ft (5–6m)
SITE Full sun
SOIL Average, free-draining
HARDINESS Z4–7 H7–1

P | *Pinus cembra* Arolla pine, Swiss stone pine

A REMARKABLY TOUGH, EVERGREEN, CONIFEROUS TREE, capable of withstanding severe cold, the arolla pine makes an attractive, formal, columnar to conical shape. The leaves provide a glossy, dark green color, but have a bluish white tinge on the inner surfaces. Cones will not appear until trees are fully mature (about 40 years old), which is a shame because they are are initially an attractive blue. Unlike many pines, this reliably grows on poor, free-draining soil, but steer clear of shady and polluted areas.

OTHER VARIETIES *P. cembra* 'Aureovariegata'; *P. cembra* 'Compacta Glauca'.

PLANT PROFILE	
HEIGHT 50–70ft (15–20m)	
SPREAD 20–25ft (6–8m)	
SITE Full sun	
SOIL Average, free-draining	
HARDINESS Z3–7 H7–1	

Pinus contorta Beach pine, Lodgepole pine, Shore pine

P

CAPABLE OF GROWING IN SANDY SOILS and even on sand dunes, which it helps bind together, the beach pine is an evergreen, coniferous tree. Initially it has a tall, loosely conical shape. In time it tends to become much more domed. The needlelike leaves are dark green, and the lower, visible part of the trunk is an attractive reddish brown. The tiny flowers (yellow males and red females) are followed by pale brown cones, sometimes with a hint of yellow. Avoid planting it in shady or polluted areas.

OTHER VARIETIES *P. contorta* var. *latifolia; P. contorta* 'Spaan's Dwarf'.

PLANT PROFILE
HEIGHT 80ft (25m)
SPREAD 25ft (8m)
SITE Full sun
SOIL Average, free-draining
HARDINESS Z6–8 H8–6

P

Pinus densiflora 'Umbraculifera' Japanese red pine

WHETHER IT FORMS A SMALL, EVERGREEN, multistemmed coniferous tree or a large bushy, shrub, 'Umbraculifera' is slow-growing and eventually achieves a width almost twice its height. The number of vertical stems is a distinct advantage because the gray bark initially has a pink, and then reddish hue. The flowers (yellow males and red females) are followed by pale brown cones, which release seeds in their second summer. Avoid shade and polluted areas.

OTHER VARIETIES *P. densiflora* 'Aurea'; *P. densiflora* 'Jane Kluis'; *P. densiflora* 'Oculus-draconis'; *P. densiflora* 'Pendula'.

PLANT PROFILE
HEIGHT 12ft (4m)
SPREAD 20ft (6m)
SITE Full sun
SOIL Average, free-draining
HARDINESS Z4–7 H7–1

Pinus nigra Austrian pine, European black pine

P

A LARGE, DOMED, EVERGREEN CONIFER, the European black pine is rated much more highly by experts as a windbreak than as an ornamental tree. And as a windbreak it is certainly impressive, even tolerating open, windy, coastal sites. *P. nigra* has fairly dense growth and foliage from low down on the trunk, and eventually makes a sizable tree, visible from quite a distance. The tiny flowers (yellow males and red females) are followed by brown cones. It does not like shady or polluted conditions.

OTHER VARIETIES *P. nigra* 'Black Prince'; *P. nigra* subsp. *laricio;* *P. nigra* subsp. *laricio* 'Bobby McGregor'; *P. nigra* subsp. *laricio* 'Globosa Viridis'; *P. nigra* subsp. *laricio* 'Moseri'.

PLANT PROFILE	
HEIGHT 100ft (30m)	
SPREAD 20–25ft (6–8m)	
SITE Full sun	
SOIL Average, free-draining	
HARDINESS Z5–8 H8–4	

P | *Pinus patula* Mexican weeping pine

AN EXTREMELY BEAUTIFUL EVERGREEN PINE, the Mexican weeping pine has nearly horizontal branches with downward-pointing clusters of fresh green, needlelike leaves, about 9in (23cm) long. They make a kind of feathery curtain, which is particularly beautiful when covered in dew, illuminated by the sun. The tiny flowers (yellow males and red females) are followed by brown cones. The young plants are frost-tender, and are best grown in mild sites or given some protection. Plant away from shade and avoid polluted areas. When flayed by cold winter winds, many leaves turn brown and drop, but this does not detract from the tree's overall appearance.

PLANT PROFILE

HEIGHT 50–70ft (15–20m)

SPREAD 20–30ft (6–10m)

SITE Full sun

SOIL Average, free-draining

HARDINESS Z8–9

Pinus radiata Monterey pine, Radiata pine

P

AN EXCELLENT CHOICE FOR A WINDBREAK, particularly on sandy soils in coastal regions, this evergreen, coniferous pine makes quick, conical growth (strangely, more impressive away from its native California). Eventually it acquires a chunky dome shape. The needlelike leaves are bright green and up to 6in (15cm) long, though some may turn brown and drop in cold, windy sites. The tiny flowers (yellow-brown males and reddish purple females) are followed by yellow-brown cones, which hang on for 20–30 years. Shade and pollution do not suit this pine.

OTHER VARIETIES *P. radiata* Aurea Group; *P. radiata* 'Marshwood'.

PLANT PROFILE
HEIGHT 80–130ft (25–40m)
SPREAD 25–40ft (8–12m)
SITE Full sun
SOIL Average, free-draining
HARDINESS Z7–9 H9–7

P | *Pinus strobus* Eastern white pine, Weymouth pine

SLENDER AND CONICAL WHEN YOUNG, this evergreen, coniferous tree becomes much more columnar as it matures (*see inset*). The needlelike leaves are gray-green and up to 5½in (14cm) long. The bark starts off gray but gradually becomes black and cracked. And the tiny flowers (yellow males and pink females) are followed by cones, which change from green to pale brown, and are up to 6in (15cm) long. There are dozens of different Eastern white pines, though most are available only from specialist nurseries. As with other pines, avoid planting in shade and polluted areas.

OTHER VARIETIES *P. strobus* 'Blue Shag'; *P. strobus* 'Fastigiata'; *P. strobus* 'Krüger's Lilliput'; *P. strobus* 'Minima'; *P. strobus* 'Radiata'.

PLANT PROFILE
HEIGHT To 120ft (35m)
SPREAD 20–25ft (6–8m)
SITE Full sun
SOIL Average, free-draining
HARDINESS Z4–9 H9–1

Pinus sylvestris Scots pine

P

WITH A TRUNK LIKE A GIANT, VERTICAL CHOPSTICK, purple-gray down low and reddish orange up high, this evergreen, coniferous tree is a familiar sight in formal landscapes. The branches spread out high up in the sky with tufty clumps of leaves (blue- or yellow-green upon closer inspection). It is much too tall for anything but the largest yard (the Scots pine was favored by garden designer Capability Brown when landscaping acres of land), where it makes a beautiful, impressive sight. There are several alternative varieties and all need sun and clean air to thrive.

OTHER VARIETIES *P. sylvestris* Aurea Group; *P. sylvestris* 'Beuvronensis'; *P. sylvestris* Fastigiata Group; *P. sylvestris* 'Gold Coin'; *P. sylvestris* 'Inverleith'; *P. sylvestris* 'Lodge Hill'; *P. sylvestris* 'Waterei'.

PLANT PROFILE		
HEIGHT 50–100ft (15–30m)		
SPREAD 20–28ft (6–9m)		
SITE Full sun		
SOIL Average, free-draining		
HARDINESS Z3–7 H7–1		

P | *Pinus wallichiana* Bhutan pine, Blue pine

GRAY-GREEN TO BLUISH GREEN, NEEDLELIKE LEAVES up to 8in (20cm) long are produced on this evergreen, coniferous tree. The tiny flowers (yellow males, blue-green and pink females) are followed by pale brown cones up to 12in (30cm) long. For the first 25 to 30 years of its life, the blue pine looks marvelous, but after that, falling branches and increasing gaps at the top mean that it may be best to replace it. For best results, avoid shade and polluted areas.

OTHER VARIETIES *P. wallichiana* 'Nana'; *P. wallichiana* 'Zebrina'.

PLANT PROFILE

HEIGHT 70–120ft (20–35m)

SPREAD 20–40ft (6–12m)

SITE Full sun

SOIL Average, free-draining

HARDINESS Z6–9 H9–5

Platanus x *hispanica* London plane

P

THOUGH IT IS CALLED THE LONDON PLANE, this tree has presumed parents that come from North America and west Asia. One of them is a long-lived giant, and their offspring makes a vigorous, deciduous, vertical tree (needing a very large lawn) with flaking brown, gray, and cream bark. The bright green leaves are up to 14in (35cm) long. It tolerates pollution well, which is why it is so often seen in English city parks and squares, but it must be kept well away from buildings. The tiny flowers are followed by clusters of brown fruits, which hang on through winter.

PLANT PROFILE	
HEIGHT 100ft (30m)	
SPREAD 70ft (20m)	
SITE Full sun	
SOIL Fertile, free-draining	
HARDINESS Z5–8 H8–5	

OTHER VARIETIES *P.* x *hispanica* 'Pyramidalis'; *P.* x *hispanica* 'Suttneri'.

P | *Platanus orientalis* Oriental plane

THE GIANT ORIENTAL PLANE needs a large space in a huge yard, where it will put on vigorous, deciduous growth. As a mature, fully grown tree, it is incredibly impressive, and has flaking gray, brown, and cream bark. The glossy green leaves are up to 10in (25cm) long. It tolerates pollution well and is a popular choice for city parks. The tiny flowers are followed by clusters of bristly brown fruits that hang on through autumn and winter.

PLANT PROFILE	
HEIGHT 100ft (30m)	
SPREAD 100ft (30m)	
SITE Full sun	
SOIL Fertile, free-draining	
HARDINESS Z7–8	

OTHER VARIETIES *P. orientalis* 'Cuneata'; *P. orientalis* f. *digitata*; *P. orientalis* 'Mirkovec'.

Platycladus orientalis Oriental arborvitae

P

MAKING AN UPRIGHT, EVERGREEN CYLINDER of vertical stems and sometimes yellowish green leaves, *P. orientalis* is best used with a battery of other conifers to create a perimeter planting. The leaves (which release a strong pine scent when crushed) often turn bronze in winter. There are many attractive forms of *P. orientalis,* including the golden yellow 'Aurea Nana', which is ideal for large rock gardens because it takes several decades to reach 10ft (3m) high, and the stiffly upright 'Elegantissima', whose leaves turn from golden yellow in summer to bronze in winter. *P. orientalis* is often sold as *Thuja orientalis*. Provide shelter from cold, drying winds.

OTHER VARIETIES *P. orientalis* 'Conspicua'; *P. orientalis* 'Meldensis'; *P. orientalis* 'Rosedalis'; *P. orientalis* 'Southport'.

PLANT PROFILE

HEIGHT To 50ft (15m)

SPREAD To 20ft (6m)

SITE Full sun

SOIL Deep, moist but free-draining

HARDINESS Z6–9 H9–6

P | *Podocarpus macrophyllus* **Kusamaki**

INITIALLY CONICAL, THEN DOMED AS IT MATURES, the evergreen, coniferous kusamaki has firm, leathery, dark green leaves, which are up to 4in (10cm) long. You need to grow a female (with flowers in green, conelike structures) in proximity to a male (with flowers in yellow, catkinlike cones) if the female is to produce its egglike, reddish purple fruits in autumn. Provide shelter from cold, drying winds, and a site that gets a decent amount of rain.

PLANT PROFILE

HEIGHT To 50ft (15m)

SPREAD 20–25ft (6–8m)

SITE Full sun

SOIL Fertile, moist but free-draining

HARDINESS Z7–11 H12–7

Podocarpus salignus Willowleaf podocarp

P

THE SLOW, GRACEFUL, EVERGREEN, CONIFEROUS GROWTH of the willowleaf podocarp is columnar or loosely conical, with spreading, downward-pointing branches covered in dark bluish green leaves, which are yellow–green beneath. Because male and female flowers are borne on separate trees, you need to grow both if the female is to produce its egglike, green or dark violet fruits in autumn. The female flowers are in green, conelike structures, while the male flowers are in yellow, catkinlike cones. Provide shelter from cold, drying winds; it prefers areas with high rainfall.

PLANT PROFILE

HEIGHT To 70ft (20m)

SPREAD 20–28ft (6–9m)

SITE Full sun

SOIL Fertile, moist but free-draining

HARDINESS Z8–11 H12–8

P

Poliothyrsis sinensis Pearl–bloom tree

A DECIDUOUS WOODLAND TREE FROM CHINA, *P. sinensis* is rarely mentioned in reference books, but it is still worth growing. The big attraction is the glossy, dark green leaves, up to 6in (15cm) long, which have a red tinge when young. The flower buds are white, and open to reveal tiny, papery, cuplike, greenish white scented flowers, which turn yellow. They appear in clusters up to 10in (25cm) long, contrasting nicely with the green foliage. Provide protection from cold, drying winds.

PLANT PROFILE
HEIGHT 30ft (10m)
SPREAD 20ft (6m)
SITE Full sun or partial shade
SOIL Fertile, free-draining
HARDINESS Z7–9

Populus alba White poplar

P

POPLARS ARE FAST-GROWING and widely used because they make good deciduous windbreaks. They can be grown virtually anywhere, from coastal regions to cities (but not near buildings), in a wide range of soils, except for the very wet. White poplar scores extra points as a windbreak (popular in sandy, coastal sites) because its leaves are dark green above and white below, creating a silvery effect in the wind. New growth shoots up from below ground level. The male and female catkins are borne on separate trees, the males being red and 3in (7cm) long, the females green and 2in (5cm) long.

OTHER VARIETIES *P. alba* f. *pyramidalis; P. alba* 'Richardii'.

PLANT PROFILE
HEIGHT 70–130ft (20–40m)
SPREAD 50ft (15m)
SITE Full sun
SOIL Fertile, moist but free-draining
HARDINESS Z3–9 H9–1

Populus balsamifera Balsam poplar, Tacamahac

THE FAST–GROWING, VERTICAL STEM is the key characteristic of this
deciduous tree. The shortish branches growing out of it tend to
angle upward. The "balsam" part of the name refers to the balsamic
scent given off by the new leaves. In early spring, the green male
and female catkins appear on separate trees. Like other poplars, it
must be grown away from buildings, especially on clay soils, because
the invasive roots suck the moisture out of the ground, which then
contracts and shrinks when dry. This can undermine foundations
and cause subsidence.

PLANT PROFILE
HEIGHT 100ft (30m)
SPREAD 25ft (8m)
SITE Full sun
SOIL Fertile, moist but free-draining
HARDINESS Z5–9 H9–5

Populus x *canadensis* 'Aurea' Canadian poplar

P

THE BIG ATTRACTION OF THIS POPLAR IS THE FOLIAGE, which starts off bronze when the leaves unfold in the spring, but turns golden yellow over summer. Make sure it is grown against a dark background to bring out an immediate, extraordinary contrast. The deciduous growth is fast, though not as fast as *P.* x *canadensis*. Red male or female catkins appear on separate plants in early spring. 'Aurea' is sometimes sold as 'Serotina Aurea'. The notes on keeping poplars away from buildings (*see opposite*) also apply here.

OTHER VARIETIES *P.* x *canadensis* 'Robusta'; *P.* x *canadensis* 'Serotina'.

PLANT PROFILE
HEIGHT 80ft (25m)
SPREAD 30ft (10m)
SITE Full sun
SOIL Fertile, moist but free-draining
HARDINESS Z5–9

P

Populus x *jackii* 'Aurora' Balm of Gilead

THE BEST REASON FOR GROWING THIS tree is the mass of new leaves in the spring, which are conspicuously marked white, cream, and pink before turning green. It is possible to grow 'Aurora' as an ornamental pillar, pruning it hard in late winter to create a formal shape, a bit like an obelisk, and to promote dense new growth with colorful leaves. Some people are snobbish about 'Aurora'—its foliage is a little like candystripe pajama fabric—but it will brighten up the spring landscape. Pruning reduces the early spring show of long, green female catkins.

PLANT PROFILE
HEIGHT 50ft (15m)
SPREAD 20ft (6m)
SITE Full sun
SOIL Fertile, moist but free-draining
HARDINESS Z4–9 H9–1

Populus nigra 'Italica' Lombardy poplar

P

INTRODUCED FROM ITALY IN THE MID-18TH CENTURY, the deciduous Lombardy poplar is a giant pencil of a tree, shooting up high and narrow, standing out for miles (*see inset*). It is often seen flanking country roads, making an aerial screen, or planted in groups. The foliage makes a wand of dark green, bronze when young, which turns yellow in autumn before falling. The early and midspring catkins are dark red.

PLANT PROFILE

HEIGHT 100ft (30m)

SPREAD 15ft (5m)

SITE Full sun

SOIL Fertile, moist but free-draining

HARDINESS Z3–9 H9–1

P

Populus tremula Quaking aspen

AN EXTRAORDINARY DECIDUOUS TREE, this aspen sends up more new suckers than most, with one particularly ancient specimen in Wales having over 1,000 stems taking up 2.5 acres (1 hectare). The dark green leaves can be late to appear, but, once they do, they will flutter and rattle in the slightest breeze, explaining the tree's common name. They turn butter yellow and fall in late autumn. A second bonus is the attractive show of male and female catkins, up to 3in (7cm) long and borne on separate trees, which hang on from the end of winter into early spring (*see inset*).

OTHER VARIETY *P. tremula* 'Pendula'.

PLANT PROFILE
HEIGHT 70ft (20m)
SPREAD 30ft (10m)
SITE Full sun
SOIL Deep, fertile, moist but free-draining
HARDINESS Z2–8 H8–1

Prunus 'Amanogawa' Ornamental cherry

P

A SUPERB FLOWERING, DECIDUOUS CHERRY, 'Amanogawa' is covered
in faintly scented, pale pink flowers in late spring. The flowers really
stand out because they open on bare branches before the leaves
appear. When the leaves unfold, they are yellowish bronze before
turning green. The autumn leaf show may feature red, yellow, and
green simultaneously. Growth is initially upright but becomes freer
and more open with age. Keep trunks clear of sprouting shoots.
Finally, note that moist but free-draining soil is very important.

OTHER VARIETIES   *P.* 'Chôshû-hizakura'; *P.* 'Spire; *P.* 'Trailblazer';
P. 'Umineko'.

PLANT PROFILE

HEIGHT 25ft (8m)

SPREAD 12ft (4m)

SITE Full sun

SOIL Average, moist but
free-draining

HARDINESS Z6–8 H8–6

P

Prunus avium 'Plena' Gean, Wild cherry

AN EXCELLENT FEATURE PLANT, and one of the tallest cherries, 'Plena' has been extremely popular for hundreds of years thanks to its superb show of double white flowers. They coincide with the midspring tulips, and make a highly effective combination with blues, reds, and the dark maroon 'Queen of Night'. An added bonus is the wild cherry's gray bark, which turns brownish red and peels. With room for just one cherry in a large yard, this is most experts' top choice. *P. avium* and 'Plena' also tolerate a wide range of soils, including thick clay.

OTHER VARIETY *P. avium* 'Stella'.

PLANT PROFILE
HEIGHT 40ft (12m)
SPREAD 40ft (12m)
SITE Full sun
SOIL Average, moist but free-draining
HARDINESS Z4–8 H8–4

Prunus cerasifera 'Nigra' Cherry plum, Myrobalan

P

THE DUAL-PURPOSE 'NIGRA' can be grown as a flowering, bushy, deciduous tree or as a hedge, both being covered by pink flowers in spring. Its big asset is the dark purple leaves (almost verging on black), which are red when they unfold in the spring. As a tall, dominating, eye-catching tree, it needs a bright background to stand out against. The flowers are usually followed by edible black or red autumn fruits.

OTHER VARIETIES *P. cerasifera* 'Hessei'; *P. cerasifera* Myrobalan Group; *P. cerasifera* 'Pissardii'; *P. cerasifera* 'Princess'; *P. cerasifera* 'Spring Glow'.

PLANT PROFILE
HEIGHT 30ft (10m)
SPREAD 30ft (10m)
SITE Full sun
SOIL Average, moist but free-draining
HARDINESS Z5–9 H9–5

P

Prunus x *cistena* Ornamental cherry

A FIRST-RATE CHOICE FOR A SMALL YARD or a flowering perimeter hedge, this ornamental cherry is slow-growing, rarely reaching above head height. It also has a lovely show of bowl-shaped white flowers right at the end of spring, when it combines well with richly colored late tulips. The cherry's flowers are sometimes followed by round, blackish purple fruits, while the leaves are initially red but gain a purple tinge over summer. *P.* x *cistena* may sometimes still be found listed in nursery catalogs as *P.* 'Crimson Dwarf'.

PLANT PROFILE

HEIGHT 5ft (1.5m)

SPREAD 5ft (1.5m)

SITE Full sun

SOIL Average, moist but free-draining

HARDINESS Z3–8 H8–1

Prunus 'Kanzan' Ornamental cherry

P

THE RICH PINK FLOWERS APPEAR IN MIDSPRING, just before or during the unfolding of the leaves. They have a light bronze-copper tinge but quickly turn green for the summer. The autumn show is equally spectacular because the leaves turn orange and yellow before falling. The branches initially tend to bend upward, creating a giant, rounded, mushroom shape. 'Kanzan' is very popular and highly reliable. Prune sprouting shoots off the trunk. Note that moist but free-draining soil is an important requirement.

OTHER VARIETIES *P.* 'Kursar'; *P.* x *subhirtella* 'Fukubana'.

PLANT PROFILE
HEIGHT 30ft (10m)
SPREAD 30ft (10m)
SITE Full sun
SOIL Average, moist but free-draining
HARDINESS Z6–8 H8–6

P

Prunus 'Kiku-shidare-zakura' Ornamental cherry

THE ARCHING, WEEPING BRANCHES are covered in bright pink double flowers in the second half of spring. They appear in dense clusters before or during the unfolding of the leaves. The latter have a bronze tinge when young, before turning green for the summer. This deciduous tree is still sometimes listed under the name 'Cheal's Weeping'. Its relatively small size makes it a very good choice for medium-sized yards. Prune sprouting shoots off the trunk. Note that moist but free-draining soil is very important.

OTHER VARIETIES *P.* 'Hally Jolivette'; *P. mume*; *P. triloba*; *P. triloba* 'Multiplex'.

PLANT PROFILE
HEIGHT 10ft (3m)
SPREAD 10ft (3m)
SITE Full sun
SOIL Average, moist but free-draining
HARDINESS Z6–8 H8–6

Prunus lusitanica 'Variegata' Portugal laurel

P

A LARGE, EVERGREEN SHRUB or tree (often used as a hedge), this laurel has dense, bushy growth packed with white-edged leaves. If left to grow unchecked, it makes a substantial flowering specimen with small, cup-shaped, scented white flowers in early summer, which stand out against the dark green leaves. The flowers are followed by red, cherrylike fruits. The Portugal laurel can also be trained with a mushroom-shaped leafy top above a bare leg, and looks very stylish in formal gardens. Note that moist but free-draining soil is very important.

OTHER VARIETIES   *P. lusitanica; P. lusitanica* subsp. *azorica;*
P. lusitanica 'Myrtifolia'.

PLANT PROFILE
HEIGHT 70ft (20m)
SPREAD 70ft (20m)
SITE Full sun
SOIL Average, moist but free-draining
HARDINESS Z7–9 H9–4

P

Prunus padus 'Watereri' Bird cherry

A TOUGH, VIGOROUS, SPREADING TREE OR SHRUB, 'Watereri'
produces clusters of lightly scented flowers that, with luck, can reach
8in (20cm) long. They are followed by small black fruits, which are
usually quickly eaten by birds. In autumn, the leaves turn pale
yellow or red before falling. Because *P. padus* is often found growing
in mountainous northern Asia, 'Watereri' and the other forms will
tolerate very poor soil. Of the cherries listed below, *P. padus*
'Colorata' is the pick of the bunch for its bronze-purple young
leaves and pink flowers.

OTHER VARIETIES *P. padus* 'Albertii'; *P. padus* 'Colorata'; *P. padus*
'Purple Queen'.

PLANT PROFILE
HEIGHT 50–60ft (15–18m)
SPREAD 30ft (10m)
SITE Full sun
SOIL Average, moist but free-draining
HARDINESS Z4–8 H8–1

Prunus 'Pink Perfection' Ornamental cherry

P

THE PINK FLOWERS APPEAR IN CLUSTERS of 3–5 at the end of spring, with some still opening at the start of summer. The buds start fattening when the bronze leaves (later green) unfold, and the flower show is generally thought to be one of the best of the ornamental cherries. The flowers are initially dark pink but they gradually fade, ending up almost white. Deciduous 'Pink Perfection' can be temperamental, so if one spring's flowering is not quite up to scratch, wait until next year. Prune sprouting shoots off the trunk. Moist but free-draining soil is very important for a healthy tree.

PLANT PROFILE
HEIGHT 25ft (8m)
SPREAD 25ft (8m)
SITE Full sun
SOIL Average, moist but free-draining
HARDINESS Z6–8 H8–6

OTHER VARIETIES *P.* 'Hillieri'; *P.* 'Jô-nioi'; *P.* 'Shirofugen'.

P

Prunus sargentii Sargent cherry

EXTREMELY HIGHLY RATED, the Sargent cherry gives a good display
in the spring and an even better one in autumn. The lavish show
of flowers makes a great aerial cloud of pink, and provides a lovely
contrast with the unfolding, reddish young leaves. The flowers are
followed by cherrylike, shiny red fruits, while the leaves turn dark
green over summer. The Sargent cherry dramatically outperforms
most of the other cherries in autumn, when the leaves turn flashy
orange-red before falling. Give it plenty of space so you can stand
back and admire it. Moist but free-draining soil is essential.

OTHER VARIETIES *P. sargentii* 'Columnaris'; *P. sargentii* 'Rancho'.

PLANT PROFILE
HEIGHT To 70ft (20m)
SPREAD 50ft (15m)
SITE Full sun
SOIL Average, moist but free-draining
HARDINESS Z5–9 H9–5

Prunus serrula Ornamental cherry

P

AN ABSOLUTELY ASTONISHING TREE due to its lustrous, copper-brown bark, which peels with age. The bark is further highlighted by the irregular, grayish horizontal rings. This cherry must be grown in a prominent position because the first thing everyone wants to do is touch it—make sure they do not have to stand on prize plants to do so. You also need good access to promptly remove any sprouting growth on the trunk. The white flowers appear in late spring, while the leaves turn yellow in autumn before falling.

OTHER VARIETIES *P. serrula* Branklyn form; *P. serrula* Dorothy Clive form.

PLANT PROFILE

HEIGHT 30ft (10m)

SPREAD 30ft (10m)

SITE Full sun

SOIL Average, moist but free-draining

HARDINESS Z6–8 H8–6

P

Prunus 'Shirotae' Ornamental cherry

THE FAINTLY SCENTED WHITE FLOWERS sometimes open before those of other ornamental cherries; if you need an early-flowering specimen, this is the one to get. The young leaves unfold pale green, turn dark green over the summer, and end up orange and red in the autumn before they fall. Growth tends to be slightly wider than it is tall, giving a spreading shape with slightly arching branches. It is still sometimes sold as 'Mount Fuji'. Prune sprouting shoots off the trunk. Moist but free-draining soil is vital.

OTHER VARIETIES *P.* 'Accolade'; *P.* 'Hillieri'; *P.* 'Jô-nioi'; *P.* 'Kursar'.

PLANT PROFILE

HEIGHT 20ft (6m)

SPREAD 25ft (8m)

SITE Full sun

SOIL Average, moist but free-draining

HARDINESS Z6–8 H8–6

Prunus x *subhirtella* 'Autumnalis Rosea' Higan cherry

P

A DECIDUOUS CHERRY WITH TWO SEASONS OF INTEREST, it has pink flowers that start opening intermittently from midautumn and carry on to spring in very mild climates. They are particularly noticeable when they open on the bare winter branches on warm days. The blooms are sometimes followed by cherrylike fruits that turn from red to black. After the last of the flowers come the young leaves, which initially have a pale bronze tinge before turning green over the summer. In autumn they turn yellow before falling. Provide moist but free-draining soil.

OTHER VARIETIES *P.* x *subhirtella* 'Autumnalis';
P. x *subhirtella* 'Fukubana'.

PLANT PROFILE
HEIGHT 25ft (8m)
SPREAD 25ft (8m)
SITE Full sun
SOIL Average, moist but free-draining
HARDINESS Z6–8 H8–6

P | *Prunus* x *subhirtella* 'Pendula Plena Rosea' Higan cherry

A VITAL INGREDIENT IN WINTER GARDENS, 'Pendula Plena Rosea'
flowers sporadically from autumn to spring in warmer regions on
tumbling, twiggy growth, giving a gentle, informal touch. It is often
grown in cottage gardens, and in Japanese-style designs, where
constant tweaking and snipping give it an elegant shape. There are
other kinds of *P.* x *subhirtella* in a variety of shapes, from the upright
to the mushroom-headed, which also flower over winter, and whose
leaves similarly turn from bronze in spring to green and then yellow
in autumn before falling.

OTHER VARIETIES *P.* x *subhirtella* 'Autumnalis'; *P.* x *subhirtella*
'Fukubana'.

PLANT PROFILE
HEIGHT 25ft (8m)
SPREAD 25ft (8m)
SITE Full sun
SOIL Average, moist but free-draining
HARDINESS Z6–8 H8–6

Prunus 'Taihaku' Great white cherry

P

THE LARGE WHITE FLOWERS open in midspring on this vigorous, deciduous, spreading tree, which ends up slightly broader than its height. The flowers are up to 2½in (6cm) wide, and make a nice contrast with the new reddish bronze leaves, which turn dark green over summer. The great white cherry is a native of Japan, but for about 200 years was thought to be extinct, until one was found growing in southern England. Now it is as popular as ever. Prune sprouting shoots off the trunk, and provide moist but free-draining soil.

OTHER VARIETIES *P.* 'Hillieri'; *P.* 'Jô-nioi'; *P.* 'Shirotae'; *P.* 'Trailblazer'.

PLANT PROFILE
HEIGHT 25ft (8m)
SPREAD 30ft (10m)
SITE Full sun
SOIL Average, moist but free-draining
HARDINESS Z6–8 H8–6

P

Prunus 'Ukon' **Ornamental cherry**

THE BEST REASON FOR CHOOSING 'UKON' is that the flowers have an unusual yellowish tinge for their first few weeks, gradually becoming white. The pink buds add to the color display, as do the leaves, which are on the bronze side when they unfold, before turning green. They change again, to red and purple, before falling in the autumn. Prune any sprouting shoots off the trunk for a cleaner, neater shape.

PLANT PROFILE
HEIGHT 25ft (8m)
SPREAD 30ft (10m)
SITE Full sun
SOIL Average, moist but free-draining
HARDINESS Z6–8 H8–6

OTHER VARIETIES *P.* 'Hillieri'; *P.* 'Jô-nioi'; *P.* 'Shirotae'; *P.* 'Trailblazer'.

Prunus x *yedoensis* Yoshino cherry

P

ALSO COMMONLY KNOWN AS THE TOKYO CHERRY because thousands are grown in that city, the Yoshino cherry is prized for its early spring show, when the graceful, arching branches, bare of leaves, are packed with gently scented, pale pink flowers that gradually fade to nearly white. They are followed by small round fruits, which darken from red to black. In the autumn the leaves turn to orange and then brownish red before falling. The name of the rarely available white form, 'Tsu-yoshino', means "bird wings," referring to its attractive, outward-pointing branches.

OTHER VARIETIES *P.* x *yedoensis* 'Ivensii';
P. x *yedoensis* 'Shidare–yoshino'.

PLANT PROFILE

HEIGHT To 50ft (15m)

SPREAD 30ft (10m)

SITE Full sun

SOIL Average, moist but free-draining

HARDINESS Z5–8 H8–5

P

Pseudolarix amabilis Golden larch

NOW BACK IN FASHION, the deciduous, coniferous golden larch needs a bit of pampering if it is to thrive and give its rich autumn show of golden–orange leaves. It is on the tender side in its first few years (when growth is slow), and it needs a sunny, sheltered site. If females are to produce brown cones, they will need an adjacent male; both produce tiny, yellow flowers. *P. amabilis* is shapely and ornamental, and well worth a place in large yards.

PLANT PROFILE

HEIGHT To 50–70ft (15–20m)

SPREAD 20–40ft (6–12m)

SITE Full sun

SOIL Fertile, free-draining, slightly acidic

HARDINESS Z5–9 H9–4

Pseudotsuga menziesii Douglas fir

P

THE FAMOUS EVERGREEN, CONIFEROUS Douglas fir has a fast-growing trunk that shoots straight up, encased in thick, corky bark that ends up reddish brown. Under a mature tree, you might have to bring your gaze up to almost three-quarters of its height before seeing the first branch. The soft leaves are dark green, and the abundant 4in- (10cm-) long cones appear after the first decade. The Douglas fir is not in any way fussy, provided the ground is not strongly alkaline.

OTHER VARIETIES *P. menziesii* 'Fastigiata'; *P. menziesii* 'Fletcheri'; *P. menziesii* 'Glauca Pendula'; *P. menziesii* 'Little Jamie'; *P. menziesii* 'Little Jon'.

PLANT PROFILE

HEIGHT 80–160ft (25–50m)

SPREAD 20–30ft (6–10m)

SITE Full sun

SOIL Average, free-draining

HARDINESS Z5–7 H7–5

P

Pterocarya fraxinifolia Caucasian wing nut

A SPLENDID, VIGOROUS, DECIDUOUS TREE, the Caucasian wing nut
needs plenty of space to spread and shoot up. There is a good show
of spring catkins, the males reaching 4½in (11cm) long and the
females 6in (15cm). They appear with the new leaves, which are up
to 16in (40cm) long and consist of up to 27 leaflets. In summer
there are nuts, each with two semicircular wings, in strings reaching
20in (50cm) long. And in autumn the glossy green leaves turn
yellow before falling. Look out for new growth shooting up from
below soil level, and promptly remove it or it will hide the trunk.

PLANT PROFILE
HEIGHT 80ft (25m)
SPREAD 70ft (20m)
SITE Full sun
SOIL Fertile, moist but free-draining
HARDINESS Z6–9 H9–6

Pterocarya stenoptera Chinese wing nut

P

A LARGE, SPREADING, DECIDUOUS TREE (*see inset*), introduced from China in the mid-19th century, the Chinese wing nut has spring catkins up to 2⅓in (6cm) long, which appear at the same time as the new leaves. The latter consist of 11 to 21 leaflets, and turn yellow in autumn before falling. In summer there are small nuts, each with two wings, in clusters reaching 12in (30cm) long. In China, it is found growing wild in moist soil, often beside streams.

PLANT PROFILE
HEIGHT 80ft (25m)
SPREAD 50ft (15m)
SITE Full sun
SOIL Fertile, moist but free-draining
HARDINESS Z7–9 H9–7

OTHER VARIETY *P. stenoptera* 'Fern Leaf'.

P | *Pterostyrax hispida* Epaulette tree

A CROSS BETWEEN A LARGE DECIDUOUS SHRUB and a spreading tree, often having multiple stems, the epaulette tree is found growing in the mountain woodlands of the Far East. Its best feature is the early summer show of lightly scented white flowers in drooping bunches. Get up close and you will also see that there is peeling, scented bark. The flowers are followed by ribbed fruits—sometimes almost large enough to look like miniature wings—with a covering of yellow-brown bristles. If necessary, prune lightly in late winter or early spring to create an attractive shape.

OTHER VARIETY *P. corymbosa.*

PLANT PROFILE

HEIGHT 50ft (15m)

SPREAD 40ft (12m)

SITE Full sun or partial shade

SOIL Deep, fertile, free-draining

HARDINESS Z5–8 H8–5

Pyrus salicifolia 'Pendula' Pear

P

THE MOUND OF SILVERY GREEN LEAVES piles up, making a big, chunky, bushy shape, just right for medium-sized yards. It is far too baggy and shapeless for formal gardens, with its downward-pointing branches, but in the right setting, the deciduous 'Pendula' has plenty of attractions. The light color of the leaves is one, as are the 8in- (20cm-) wide clusters of creamy white flowers, which are followed by pear-shaped green fruits. The parent, *P. salicifolia*, is much taller and more upright, reaching 25ft (8m) high.

PLANT PROFILE	
HEIGHT 15ft (5m)	
SPREAD 12ft (4m)	
SITE Full sun	
SOIL Average, free-draining	
HARDINESS Z5–9 H9–5	

Q | *Quercus cerris* 'Argenteovariegata' Turkey oak

AN OAK WITH A DIFFERENCE, the Turkey oak has young unfolding leaves that are rich green with yellow around the margins. They turn creamy white and finally yellow-brown in autumn before they drop. If you find any stems producing all-green young leaves, cut them off or the whole tree might eventually lose its attractive variegation. The acorns are in frizzy-looking cups, covered in long scales (*see inset*). It is more of a woodland or mini arboretum tree than a specimen grown for its shape and beauty. Like other Turkey oaks, it is quite happy on poor soil. 'Argenteovariegata' is still sometimes sold as *Q. cerris* 'Variegata'.

OTHER VARIETIES *Q. cerris*; *Q. cerris* 'Wodan'.

PLANT PROFILE
HEIGHT 50ft (15m)
SPREAD 40ft (12m)
SITE Sun or partial shade
SOIL Deep, fertile, free-draining
HARDINESS Z7–9 H9–7

Quercus coccinea Scarlet oak

THE SCARLET AUTUMN LEAVES ARE THE BIG ATTRACTION of the scarlet oak, whose dark green foliage turns a flamboyant red before falling. It prefers lighter rather than heavier ground and is not quite as solidly massive as some oaks but has a slightly more delicate air. The male flowers are yellow-green catkins and the females are inconspicuous, followed by acorns enclosed in cups.

OTHER VARIETY *Q. coccinea* 'Splendens'.

PLANT PROFILE
HEIGHT 70ft (20m)
SPREAD 50ft (15m)
SITE Full sun or partial shade
SOIL Light, fertile, free-draining, acidic
HARDINESS Z5–9 H9–4

Q | *Quercus frainetto* Hungarian oak

A SUPERB, FAST-GROWING, DECIDUOUS TREE, this is a quintessential oak. It puts on big, dense growth with thick branches and dark green leaves, characterized by rounded zigzag edges, up to 8in (20cm) long. In autumn they turn yellow-brown before falling. The catkins (yellow-green males and inconspicuous females) are followed by acorns, half-enclosed in cups.

OTHER VARIETY *Q. frainetto* 'Hungarian Crown'.

PLANT PROFILE
HEIGHT 100ft (30m)
SPREAD 70ft (20m)
SITE Full sun or partial shade
SOIL Fertile, free-draining
HARDINESS Z5–8 H8–1

Quercus ilex Holm oak

Q

THE GREAT BRITISH OAK could be another name for this tree, which has been widely grown in the British Isles for hundreds of years. It is a massive, solid tree with dark gray bark, verging on black, and dark green leaves that are rigid and leathery. The catkins (yellow males and inconspicuous females) are followed by acorns enclosed in cups. It is considered best to plant holm oaks in mild or coastal regions (where they block and withstand buffeting winds), avoiding particularly cold, inland sites.

PLANT PROFILE	
HEIGHT 80ft (25m)	
SPREAD 70ft (20m)	
SITE Full sun or partial shade	
SOIL Fertile, free-draining	
HARDINESS Z4–8 H9–2	

Q | *Quercus palustris* Pin oak

A FAST-GROWING, CHUNKY GIANT OF A TREE, the pin oak is tolerant of flood plains and wet ground, and even city streets, where it reliably produces a superb, impressive crown. It also has large, shiny leaves, deeply divided into seven sections, which flare up in the autumn when they turn bright, rich (or brownish) red and dominate the landscape. A native of the eastern parts of North America, it does well in long, hot summers.

OTHER VARIETY *Q. palustris* 'Pendula'.

PLANT PROFILE
HEIGHT 70ft (20m)
SPREAD 40ft (12m)
SITE Sun or partial shade
SOIL Deep, fertile, free-draining
HARDINESS Z5–8 H8–5

Quercus petraea Sessile oak

Q

A DECIDUOUS BRITISH SPECIES, thought to pre-date the English oak (*Q. robur, see page 258*) in the UK, it is also the experts' top choice. It may not grow quite as high as *Q. robur* but it does tolerate lighter soil (avoid heavy clay), and its overall shape is more aesthetically satisfying. The late spring catkins (yellow-green males and inconspicuous females) are followed by acorns enclosed in cups.

PLANT PROFILE
HEIGHT 100ft (30m)
SPREAD 80ft (25m)
SITE Full sun or partial shade
SOIL Fertile, free-draining
HARDINESS Z5–8 H8–5

OTHER VARIETIES *Q. petraea* 'Insecata'; *Q. petraea* 'Purpurea'.

Q | *Quercus robur* **English oak**

A GIANT, RUGGED, DECIDUOUS TREE, and a British native, this oak is commonly found on clay soils and puts on wide-spreading, rounded growth. The leaves are dark green above with a bluish tinge beneath, and have 3–6 rounded sections on each side and a very short stalk. The late spring catkins (yellow-green males and inconspicuous females) are followed by acorns enclosed in cups.

OTHER VARIETIES   *Q. robur* 'Argenteomarginata'; *Q. robur* 'Concordia'; *Q. robur* f. *fastigiata; Q. robur* 'Pendula'; *Q. robur* 'Purpurascens'.

PLANT PROFILE

HEIGHT 35m (120ft)

SPREAD 80ft (25m)

SITE Full sun or partial shade

SOIL Fertile, free-draining, likes clay

HARDINESS Z5–8 H8–3

Quercus rubra Red oak

FAST-GROWING AND DECIDUOUS, this North American oak has a big reputation for its beautiful autumn leaf color. On mature trees the leaves first turn yellow and then reddish brown, though on young ones they might turn red right away. The catkins (yellow-green males and inconspicuous females) are followed by acorns enclosed in cups.

PLANT PROFILE

HEIGHT 80ft (25m)

SPREAD 70ft (20m)

SITE Full sun or partial shade

SOIL Fertile, free-draining, acidic

HARDINESS Z5–9 H9–5

OTHER VARIETIES *Q. rubra* 'Aurea'; *Q. rubra* 'Sunshine'.

Q | *Quercus suber* Cork oak

THE CORK OAK MAKES A FINE EVERGREEN TREE with dark green leaves, provided it is well protected from exposed sites with cold, icy winds. It is best known because it is grown on huge plantations, mainly in Portugal and Spain, where it provides the cork for sealing wine bottles (obtained from the thick layer of soft bark, without causing any damage). The cork oak's days as a commercial tree look numbered as wine producers switch to synthetic stoppers in order to eliminate corked (spoiled) wine, which costs the industry huge amounts of money every year.

PLANT PROFILE

HEIGHT 70ft (20m)

SPREAD 70ft (20m)

SITE Full sun

SOIL Deep, fertile, free-draining

HARDINESS Z7–9 H9–7

Rhus typhina **Staghorn sumac, Velvet sumac**

SHRUBBY AND MULTISTEMMED, this sumac gives a sensational autumn display. The dangling green leaves on each branch, like rows of miniature flags, each one up to 24in (60cm) long, turn flashy orange-red before falling. Other attractions include the highly attractive, reddish new stems, which have a soft, furry covering said to look like stags' antlers. The summer flowers are yellow-green and appear in erect, conical clusters (*see inset*); they are followed by deep red fruits. This tree can also be grown as a large shrub, but it is very bare over winter. If pruning, note that the sap can be an irritant.

OTHER VARIETY *R. typhina* 'Dissecta'.

PLANT PROFILE
HEIGHT 15ft (5m) or more
SPREAD 20ft (6m)
SITE Full sun
SOIL Average, moist but free-draining
HARDINESS Z3–8 H8–1

R | *Robinia pseudoacacia* 'Frisia' Black locust, False acacia

THE YELLOW-GREEN LEAVES are the best reason for choosing the deciduous, fast-growing 'Frisia'. When they unfold in the spring they are actually golden yellow, and they fire up orange-yellow before falling in autumn. The tree's upright shape is another attraction, being irregularly columnar (*see inset*). The sparse, tiny white flowers are insignificant, and appear in hanging clusters.

PLANT PROFILE
HEIGHT 50ft (15m)
SPREAD 25ft (8m)
SITE Full sun
SOIL Average, moist but free-draining
HARDINESS Z4–9 H9–1

OTHER VARIETIES *R. pseudoacacia*; *R. pseudoacacia* 'Bessoniana'; *R. pseudoacacia* TWISTY BABY ('Lace Lady'); *R. pseudoacacia* 'Umbraculifera'.

Robinia pseudoacacia 'Tortuosa' Black locust, False acacia

R

'TORTUOSA' SCORES EVEN HIGHER POINTS than its parent, *R. pseudoacacia*, purely because it has slightly more ornamental, twisted, contorted stems. It is also relatively slow growing, but otherwise has all the same attributes—the green leaves turn orange–yellow before falling in autumn, and the upright shape is attractively, irregularly columnar. The sparse, tiny white flowers are also insignificant, and appear in hanging clusters.

PLANT PROFILE
HEIGHT 50ft (15m)
SPREAD 30ft (10m)
SITE Full sun
SOIL Average, moist but free-draining
HARDINESS Z4–9 H9–3

OTHER VARIETIES *R. pseudoacacia*; *R. pseudoacacia* 'Bessoniana'.

Salix alba var. *sericea* Silver willow

A BEAUTIFUL SIGHT IN EARLY SUMMER, when its silver-gray leaves unfold and get blown around in the wind, the silver willow thrives in meadows and by the banks of streams. It is smaller and slower-growing than the related *S. alba*, but nevertheless makes a fine, tall, round-headed specimen. To highlight the light color of the leaves, ensure that there is a background of dark green in the distance. The pick of the varieties below is *S. alba* subsp. *vitellina* 'Britzensis', which has bright orange-red young shoots over the winter months, making a striking tracery against the sky. Prune it hard every other year to promote colorful new growth.

OTHER VARIETIES *S. alba* 'Dart's Snake'; *S. alba* 'Tristis'; *S. alba* subsp. *vitellina* 'Britzensis'.

PLANT PROFILE
HEIGHT 50ft (15m)
SPREAD 25ft (8m)
SITE Full sun
SOIL Deep, moist but free-draining
HARDINESS Z4–9 H9–1

Salix babylonica Weeping willow

S

A GREAT ROUNDED TREE, this was the original weeping willow before others started grabbing their share of the market. It has green leaves with a grayish tinge underneath, and silvery green catkins in the spring. The dragon's claw willow, *S. babylonica* var. *pekinensis* 'Tortuosa' (*see inset*), is even more striking with its twisting, corkscrewing stems, which really stand out in winter when the leaves have fallen. Note that because the roots of both are invasive and water-seeking, the planting hole must be dug well away from pipes and buildings; this is especially important if the soil is clay because, as the roots suck out the moisture, the soil promptly dries and shrinks.

OTHER VARIETY *S. x sepulcralis* var. *chrysocoma*.

PLANT PROFILE
HEIGHT 40ft (12m)
SPREAD 40ft (12m)
SITE Full sun
SOIL Moist but free-draining
HARDINESS Z6–9 H9–1

S

Salix caprea 'Kilmarnock' **Kilmarnock willow**

AN EXCELLENT CHOICE FOR SMALL YARDS, this miniature, deciduous willow rarely hits 10ft (3m) high, and has stiff, downward-pointing stems that make an umbrella shape. It catches the eye in the second half of spring, when the gray catkins, studded with yellow, appear down the full length of the bare stems, some almost touching the ground. They are followed by dark green leaves that are gray-green on the underside. Prune the top of the tree annually in late winter to stop it from getting too congested.

PLANT PROFILE
HEIGHT 5–6ft (1.5–2m)
SPREAD 6ft (2m)
SITE Full sun
SOIL Moist but free-draining
HARDINESS Z6–8 H8–6

Salix daphnoides Violet willow

S

AN EXTREMELY EFFECTIVE WILLOW, this tree initially tends to grow straight upward, then fills out and spreads. The young violet-purple shoots are a key feature because in the early stages of winter they are covered by white blooms, which are gradually knocked off. By giving *S. daphnoides* a hard pruning every other year in midspring, you promote a fresh supply of these colorful shoots. In late winter and early spring, the silky gray catkins appear just before the leaves open (the male catkins have yellow pollen). The violet willow grows wild throughout central Europe.

PLANT PROFILE

HEIGHT 25ft (8m)

SPREAD 20ft (6m)

SITE Full sun

SOIL Deep, moist but free-draining

HARDINESS Z5–9 H9–5

S | *Salix* 'Erythroflexuosa' Willow

A HIGHLY ATTRACTIVE, SPREADING, DECIDUOUS TREE with arching
branches, it combines the best of its parents, the golden weeping
willow (*see page 272*) and the dragon's claw willow (*see page 265*).
The result is spiraling, twisting shoots that are initially orange-
yellow, and really stand out in winter when they are bare and
leafless. When the leaves appear in the spring, they too are twisted,
and are mid-green on top and slightly bluish beneath. The leaves
coincide with the slender, pale yellow catkins.

.

PLANT PROFILE

HEIGHT 15ft (5m)

SPREAD 15ft (5m)

SITE Full sun

SOIL Moist but free-
draining

HARDINESS Z5–9 H9–5

Salix exigua Coyote willow

S

GROWN FOR ITS BEAUTIFUL SHOW of fluttering, gray-green leaves in summer, which start off sage green in the spring, the coyote willow is theoretically more of a shrub than a tree, but it does produce tall, upright, screening growth with a mass of stems firing out of the ground. It is often used to support, and provide an effective color contrast with, dark-colored rambling roses. Though moist soil is ideal, *S. exigua* will also thrive in poor, dry, stony ground. In the latter conditions, do not try growing roses through it.

PLANT PROFILE

HEIGHT 12ft (4m)

SPREAD 15ft (5m)

SITE Full sun

SOIL Deep, moist but free-draining

HARDINESS Z4–6 H6–1

S

Salix integra 'Hakuro-nishiki' Willow

MAKING A SMALL, DECIDUOUS TREE OR LARGE SHRUB, 'Hakuro-nishiki' gets the spring off to a good start. There are thin catkins on the bare branches, followed by the pretty pink and white leaves. If it is placed in full sun, there is a chance that the foliage will burn, so a degree of light shade, especially at midday, is important. Since the pink of the leaves immediately catches the eye, make sure 'Hakuro-nishiki' is given a prominent position. Grow it in Japanese-style gardens and by ponds.

PLANT PROFILE
HEIGHT 10ft (3m)
SPREAD 10ft (3m)
SITE Sun or light dappled shade
SOIL Moist but free-draining
HARDINESS Z5–7

Salix purpurea 'Pendula' Purple osier

S

WHEN TRAINED AS A STANDARD, with a sturdy, single, upright stem, the purple osier makes a very attractive small tree with long, drooping, dangling branches. The young shoots are a bonus because they often have a red tinge, while the leaves are green above with a bluish tinge beneath. The related *S. purpurea* has more of a shrubby appearance, though it too has arching branches and often the same red-tinged young shoots. On both plants, the silver-gray catkins appear before the leaves start unfolding.

OTHER VARIETY *S. purpurea* 'Nana'.

PLANT PROFILE

HEIGHT 15ft (5m)

SPREAD 15ft (5m)

SITE Full sun

SOIL Deep, moist but free-draining

HARDINESS Z3–9

S | *Salix* x *sepulcralis* var. *chrysocoma* Golden weeping willow

A STAR AMONG THE WILLOWS, it forms a fast-growing, striking, weeping shape with a mass of dangling golden yellow twigs (no other salix can rival this golden yellow). The effect is highlighted by planting golden weeping willow in the open where it is well lit by the sun. The catkins appear in spring at the same time as the leaves. The only note of caution is that it can be attacked by scab and canker. Make sure these disorders are not prevalent in your area before planting. If they are, go for the disease-resistant, 60ft- (20m-) high *S.* x *pendulina* var. *elegantissima.*

PLANT PROFILE

HEIGHT 50ft (15m)

SPREAD 50ft (15m)

SITE Full sun

SOIL Deep, moist but free-draining

HARDINESS Z6–9 H9–6

Sassafras albidum

ANYONE WHO SPENDS AUTUMN IN PENNSYLVANIA will want to light up their own yard with the rip-roaring bonanza of yellow, then orange and purple autumn leaves produced by *S. albidum*. The mixture of leaf shapes is also attractive. If you grow a male near a female, the latter produces small, dark blue fruits. The best place to grow *S. albidum* is in, or at the edge of, a woodland garden. Promptly remove any growth emerging from below ground level.

PLANT PROFILE

HEIGHT 80ft (25m)

SPREAD 50ft (15m)

SITE Full sun or partial shade

SOIL Average, rich, moist but free-draining, acidic

HARDINESS Z4–8 H8–3

S

Saxegothaea conspicua **Prince Albert's yew**

THIS EVERGREEN, DECIDUOUS CONIFER is not actually a yew; the
bark certainly has similarities, but that is about it. What you do get
from this South American small tree or large shrub (it is bushy
when grown in cold areas) is loose, tumbling growth covered in
dark green leaves, which have two silver bands on the undersides.
The male cones are dark purple, and the prickly females are
glaucous green. Provide shelter from cold, drying winds, possibly
growing it in a woodland garden. It tolerates light shade.

PLANT PROFILE
HEIGHT To 70ft (20m)
SPREAD 15–25ft (5–8m)
SITE Full sun or partial shade
SOIL Average, free-draining, slightly acidic
HARDINESS Z8–10 H10–8

Sciadopitys verticillata Japanese umbrella pine

S

THE TWIN ADVANTAGES OF the almost pyramidal, evergreen, coniferous umbrella pine are the colored bark and the whorls of thin, spindly leaves. The bark is reddish brown and peels in vertical ribbons, while the leaves, on close inspection, are like clusters of giant spider's legs sticking outwards. The flowers (yellow males and green females) are followed by reddish brown cones. Some trees can be hidden away to provide a combined effect, but this one is so attractive it needs to be highlighted in an open position.

OTHER VARIETIES *S. verticillata* 'Firework'; *S. verticillata* 'Golden Rush'; *S. verticillata* 'Pygmy'.

PLANT PROFILE
HEIGHT 30–70ft (10–20m)
SPREAD To 20–25ft (6–8m)
SITE Full sun or partial shade
SOIL Average, moist but free-draining, slightly acidic
HARDINESS Z5–9 H9–4

S *Sequoia sempervirens* Coast redwood

A COAST REDWOOD IS THE TALLEST TREE IN THE WORLD, once measured at 368ft (112m) high, but you are not likely to rival this in the average backyard—and even if you do, you will not be around to celebrate. This is a stupendous, evergreen tree with an upward-thrusting central trunk encased in thick, spongy bark (*see inset*). The late-winter to early-spring flowers are followed by reddish brown cones. Make sure that it is not hidden away.

OTHER VARIETIES *S. sempervirens* 'Adpressa'; *S. sempervirens* 'Prostrata'.

PLANT PROFILE
HEIGHT 70–100ft (20–30m)
SPREAD 20–28ft (6–9m)
SITE Full sun to light, dappled shade
SOIL Average, moist but free-draining
HARDINESS Z8–9 H9–8

Sophora japonica Japanese pagoda tree

AN INTERESTING CHOICE FOR A JAPANESE GARDEN (though it actually comes from China and Korea), the Japanese pagoda tree is a tall, spreading, deciduous tree. The covering of foliage seems to have a wonderfully layered effect because the leaves actually consist of up to 17 leaflets, which are glossy and dark green, turning yellow in autumn. Given a long, hot summer, the tiny white flowers appear on mature trees in late summer and early autumn, but you are unlikely to get any fruits.

PLANT PROFILE	
HEIGHT To 100ft (30m)	
SPREAD 70ft (20m)	
SITE Full sun	
SOIL Average, free-draining	
HARDINESS Z5–9 H9–1	

OTHER VARIETY *S. japonica* 'Pendula'.

S

Sorbus aria 'Lutescens' Whitebeam

'LUTESCENS' IS HIGHLY RATED because of the silvery gray, feltlike covering on the new spring leaves, which later turn gray-green. In autumn they turn red or yellow before falling. The late-spring white flowers are followed by dark red berries with brown speckling. 'Lutescens' is a good choice because it has compact growth and is a robust, no-nonsense tree that withstands a wide range of conditions, including city pollution, heavy clay, and exposed coastal positions.

OTHER VARIETIES   *S. aria* 'Chrysophylla'; *S. aria* 'Magnifica'; *S. aria* 'Majestica'.

PLANT PROFILE
HEIGHT 30ft (10m)
SPREAD 25ft (8m)
SITE Full sun or light, dappled shade
SOIL Average, humus-rich, free-draining
HARDINESS Z6–8 H8–6

Sorbus aucuparia Mountain ash, Rowan

S

THE LATE-SUMMER TO AUTUMN SHOW is the mountain ash at its best—you get clusters of bright orange-red berries set against the dark green leaves, consisting of up to 12 leaflets. The berries appear in huge numbers, and last into winter, attracting hungry birds. They are at their most beautiful on sunny days, and when they start appearing out of the autumn mists. An added bonus comes later in autumn, when the leaves turn red or yellow before falling. The white flowers appear in late spring. The deciduous mountain ash tolerates city conditions and acidic soil.

OTHER VARIETIES *S. aucuparia* 'Aspleniifolia'; *S. aucuparia* 'Dirkenii'; *S. aucuparia* 'Fastigiata'; *S. aucuparia* 'Sheerwater Seedling'; *S. aucuparia* var. *xanthocarpa*.

PLANT PROFILE
HEIGHT 50ft (15m)
SPREAD 22ft (7m)
SITE Full sun or light, dappled shade
SOIL Average, humus-rich, free-draining
HARDINESS Z2–7 H7–1

S | *Sorbus cashmiriana* Kashmir rowan

THE BRIGHT WHITE, MARBLELIKE BERRIES (initially with a pink tinge) make this a good choice to place beside a red-berrying sorbus for maximum contrast. And the white berries hang on long after the leaves have fallen because the birds tend to leave them alone. The deciduous leaves, consisting of 17–21 leaflets, are another attraction. They have a bluish tinge beneath, and turn yellow or red before they fall in autumn. Clusters of the white flowers open in late spring. Growth is modest and open, making it ideal for small to medium-sized yards.

OTHER VARIETY *S. cashmiriana* 'Rosiness'.

PLANT PROFILE
HEIGHT 25ft (8m)
SPREAD 22ft (7m)
SITE Full sun or light, dappled shade
SOIL Average, humus-rich, free-draining
HARDINESS Z5–7 H7–5

Sorbus commixta Japanese rowan

THIS FAR EASTERN, BROADLY CONICAL tree or shrub is grown not so much for its late spring show of white flowers as for its clusters of bright orange-red or red berries, which appear from late summer and are quickly taken by birds. The autumn leaf change is even better—the colors switch from green to yellow, and then go up a gear to red or purple. Give *S. commixta* a prominent position in a large lawn, or include it in a colorful border plan.

OTHER VARIETY *S. commixta* 'Embley'.

PLANT PROFILE

HEIGHT 30ft (10m)

SPREAD 22ft (7m)

SITE Full sun or light, dappled shade

SOIL Average, humus-rich, free-draining

HARDINESS Z6–8 H8–6

S | *Sorbus domestica* Service tree

COMING HIGH ON THE LIST of very useful sorbuses, the service tree stands out because of its berries, flowers, leaves, and bark. The 1¼in-(3cm-) wide berries (considered edible long ago, and once used to make a kind of cider) are either round or pear-shaped, and yellow-green with a red flush. They follow the wide clusters of white flowers. The green leaves turn yellow or orange-red in autumn before falling, and the rich brown bark is quite rough and ridged. The sticky winter buds are another plus.

PLANT PROFILE

HEIGHT 70ft (20m)

SPREAD 40ft (12m)

SITE Full sun or light, dappled shade

SOIL Average, humus-rich, free-draining

HARDINESS Z6–8

Sorbus hupehensis var. *obtusa* Hubei rowan

S

ALSO KNOWN AS THE CHINESE MOUNTAIN ASH, the Hubei rowan provides a decent array of colors. The leaves are silvery gray-green above, with a bluish tinge underneath, and then turn bright, brash red in autumn. The flowers are white, appearing in clusters in late spring. And the berries end up dark pink, hanging on for a long time (usually being ignored by the birds), into the first half of winter. If you prefer slightly pink-tinged white berries, go for the related *S. hupehensis*, introduced from China in 1910.

PLANT PROFILE
HEIGHT To 25ft (8m)
SPREAD To 25ft (8m)
SITE Full sun or light, dappled shade
SOIL Average, humus-rich, free-draining
HARDINESS Z3–8 H8–1

S | *Sorbus intermedia* Swedish whitebeam

ITS COMPACT, ROUNDED SHAPE makes the deciduous Swedish whitebeam a very good choice for medium-sized yards, where it comes alive in late spring with 5in- (12cm-) wide clusters of white flowers, followed in the summer by attractive bright red berries. The dark green leaves tend to be silvery underneath. Swedish whitebeam is a good choice for a specimen tree or, when planted in numbers, creating a buffer or "wall" to keep out the wind, since it tolerates periods of severe weather better than many broad-leaved trees.

OTHER VARIETY *S. intermedia* 'Brouwers'.

PLANT PROFILE
HEIGHT 40ft (12m)
SPREAD 40ft (12m)
SITE Full sun or light, dappled shade
SOIL Average, humus-rich, free-draining
HARDINESS Z5–8 H8–3

Sorbus 'Joseph Rock' Rowan

S

ONE OF THE BEST SORBUSES, the deciduous 'Joseph Rock' has sensational autumn color. The leaves (consisting of up to 21 leaflets) fire up orange, red, and purple, and in addition, you get pale yellow berries that turn bright orange–yellow. If your garden needs an injection of aerial color, this is a first-rate choice. The spring flowers are white. 'Joseph Rock' is also valued because it tolerates different conditions, ranging from light, sandy soils to heavier ground. If blackened leaves appear (a sign of fireblight), cut back the affected growth in summer to 2ft (60cm) below the diseased area.

PLANT PROFILE

HEIGHT 30ft (10m)

SPREAD 22ft (7m)

SITE Full sun or light, dappled shade

SOIL Average, humus-rich, free-draining

HARDINESS Z7–8 H8–7

S | *Sorbus koehneana* Rowan

A SMALL, SPREADING TREE OR LARGE, BUSHY SHRUB, this sorbus is
a highly attractive plant for the medium-sized yard, where gentle
summer pruning can help impart an elegant shape. Its other virtues
include dark green leaves, and the late-spring, drooping clusters of
white flowers that produce small, round green berries, which
gradually ripen to white. It was introduced from China in 1910.
For a similar, even smaller sorbus, try *S. fruticosa,* which rarely gets
above head-height, and can be grown in tubs on patios with an
underplanting of spring bulbs.

PLANT PROFILE
HEIGHT 15ft (5m)
SPREAD 20ft (6m)
SITE Full sun or light, dappled shade
SOIL Average, humus-rich, free-draining
HARDINESS Z6–8

Sorbus sargentiana Sargent rowan

MAKING A LARGE, SUBSTANTIAL DECIDUOUS TREE, *S. sargentiana* is grown for one main reason: the leaves, consisting of up to 13 leaflets, turn flamboyant red and orange in autumn (in some years, the show may be on the poor side, but don't let that discourage you). At the same time, it also has small, bright red berries in large clusters up to 8in (20cm) wide. In the spring there are clusters of white flowers. The final attraction is given by the winter flower buds, which are big, fat, and red, and leak a sticky resin.

PLANT PROFILE

HEIGHT 30ft (10m)

SPREAD 30ft (10m)

SITE Full sun or light, dappled shade

SOIL Average, humus-rich, free-draining

HARDINESS Z5–7 H7–5

S | *Sorbus scalaris* Rowan

WITH SUFFICIENT ROOM, *S. scalaris* makes a superb tree that comes alive in late autumn, when it is upgraded into a mass of bright red and purple foliage, before the leaves drop. Other attractions are the late-spring and early-summer show of white flowers, and the small, round, shiny red berries, which appear over the summer months. It needs plenty of space because it does tend to spread out, which is why it is often used as part of a hedge or as a feature tree in a wild garden. *S. scalaris* was discovered in China in the early 20th century.

PLANT PROFILE
HEIGHT 30ft (10m)
SPREAD 30ft (10m)
SITE Full sun or light, dappled shade
SOIL Average, humus-rich, free-draining
HARDINESS Z6–8 H8–6

Sorbus vilmorinii Vilmorin rowan

AN APT CHOICE FOR A MEDIUM-SIZED YARD, this small, deciduous tree or large shrub has two seasons of interest. White flowers appear in spring, in clusters about 4in (10cm) wide, and in autumn, more spectacularly, the leaves turn red and purple. The leaves consist of about 30 leaflets and, over summer, are dark green with a hint of gray. The fruits following the flowers turn from red through various shades of pink, ending up nearly white. In large yards it may be best to grow *S. vilmorinii* in groups of three for increased impact.

PLANT PROFILE
HEIGHT 15ft (5m)
SPREAD 15ft (5m)
SITE Full sun or light, dappled shade
SOIL Average, humus-rich, free-draining
HARDINESS Z6–8 H8–6

S | *Staphylea holocarpa* 'Rosea' Bladdernut

AN UPRIGHT, DECIDUOUS SMALL TREE or large shrub, 'Rosea' puts on a delicate spring show. Unlike its parent, *S. holocarpa*, which has white flowers, 'Rosea' has pink blooms which appear before the leaves. When the leaves, consisting of 3 leaflets, finally unfold, they are bronze and later turn bluish green. They, in turn, are followed by greenish white fruits. The bladdernut is usually grown in woodland gardens or among other shrubs.

OTHER VARIETY *S. holocarpa* var. *rosea*.

PLANT PROFILE
HEIGHT 30ft (10m)
SPREAD 20ft (6m)
SITE Full sun or partial shade
SOIL Average, moist but free-draining
HARDINESS Z6–9 H9–6

Stewartia pseudocamellia Japanese stewartia

S

AN EXCELLENT MULTIPURPOSE DECIDUOUS TREE, *S. pseudocamellia* has three key attractions. First, the bark perks up winter landscapes with its reddish brown color, on top of which grow patches of purple that keep peeling off to reveal areas of orange beneath. Second, the dark green leaves put on a lively autumn show when they turn yellow-orange and red. And third, there are roselike, cup-shaped white flowers in midsummer, up to 2½in (6cm) across, with creamy yellow in the middle.

OTHER VARIETY *S. pseudocamellia* Koreana Group.

PLANT PROFILE
HEIGHT 70ft (20m)
SPREAD 25ft (8m)
SITE Full sun or light, dappled shade
SOIL Average, humus-rich, moist but free-draining
HARDINESS Z5–8 H8–1

S

Stewartia sinensis Chinese stewartia

THREE SEASONS OF INTEREST are provided by *S. sinensis*, starting with the summer flowers. They are scented, white, cup-shaped, and roselike, and are usually 2in (5cm) wide. In autumn, the dark green leaves turn brilliant red before falling. And the reddish brown bark peels and flakes to reveal patches of gray and cream beneath, adding winter interest (*see inset*). Provide shelter from strong winds. This tree was introduced from China at the start of the 20th century.

PLANT PROFILE

HEIGHT 70ft (20m)

SPREAD 22ft (7m)

SITE Full sun or light, dappled shade

SOIL Average, humus-rich, moist but free-draining

HARDINESS Z5–8 H8–5

Styrax hemsleyanus Hemsley snowbell

S

AN OPEN, DECIDUOUS CHINESE TREE or shrubby bush, *S. hemsleyanus* is grown for its show of bell-shaped white flowers, with distinctive yellow stamens within. Because they appear in early summer, they add useful aerial color between the end of the spring bulbs and the start of the beds and borders. In the wild, *S. hemsleyanus* is found growing in open woodlands, where conditions are cool and the ground is often damp. The key to success in gardens is making sure that the tree is well protected from blasts of cold, drying winds.

PLANT PROFILE

HEIGHT 25ft (8m)

SPREAD 15ft (5m)

SITE Full sun or partial shade

SOIL Fertile, humus-rich, moist but free-draining, neutral to acidic

HARDINESS Z7–9

S *Styrax obassia* Fragrant snowbell

A DELIGHTFUL, FLOWERING DECIDUOUS TREE for the start of summer, the fragrant snowbell is named for its lengths of bell-shaped, lightly scented white flowers that hang like pendants on dangling chains. The flowers resemble snowdrops, and are nicely set off by the dark green foliage, which is bluish gray beneath, and eventually turns yellow before dropping in autumn. In the wild, it grows in open woodlands, in light shade, beneath trees towering even higher. It is therefore important to provide moist soil, dappled shade, and shelter from the wind.

PLANT PROFILE

HEIGHT 40ft (12m)

SPREAD 22ft (7m)

SITE Full sun or partial shade

SOIL Fertile, humus-rich, moist but free-draining

HARDINESS Z6–8 H8–6

Tamarix ramosissima 'Pink Cascade' Tamarisk

T

A SMALL DECIDUOUS TREE OR GRACEFUL SHRUB, with a lot of new shoots from below ground level, 'Pink Cascade' is grown for its leaves and flowers. The former are light, feathery, and needlelike, with a lovely, airy effect. But they are practically hidden in late summer, when the plant is covered in a profusion of pink flowers on the new growth. It can be planted in as a windbreak in coastal regions, where it tolerates blustery but moisture-filled winds, or inland, where it needs a sheltered position away from cold, drying winds. When growing it as a hedging windbreak, cut it back hard in the spring to encourage plenty of new, strong growth.

OTHER VARIETY *T. ramosissima* 'Rubra'.

PLANT PROFILE	
HEIGHT 15ft (5m)	
SPREAD 15ft (5m)	
SITE Full sun	
SOIL Average, moist	
HARDINESS Z3–8 H8–1	

T

Taxodium distichum Swamp cypress

THE SWAMP CYPRESS IS a large, deciduous, columnar conifer (*see inset*) with fresh, green summer growth followed by lovely orange-brown and rust red hues in autumn. Over winter, the bare branches are rather gaunt against the sky. The tiny flowers (the males are yellow-green, females green) appear in catkins, which develop in autumn but open the following spring. They are followed by cones that turn from green to brown. Despite the "swamp" part of the common name, *T. distichum* does not have to be grown in standing water, as long as the soil is moist and, ideally, acidic.

OTHER VARIETIES *T. distichum* var. *imbricatum; T. distichum* var. *imbricatum* 'Nutans'; *T. distichum* 'Secrest'.

PLANT PROFILE
HEIGHT 70–130ft (20–40m)
SPREAD 20–28ft (6–9m)
SITE Full sun or partial shade
SOIL Moist to wet, acidic
HARDINESS Z5–11 H12–5

Taxus baccata 'Fastigiata' Florence Court yew, Irish yew

A DENSE, UPRIGHT, EVERGREEN COLUMN of dark green leaves (*see inset*), the Irish yew adds a vertical shape on large, flat lawns, and is particularly useful where it flanks paths or stands at the entrance to another part of the yard. Gentle trimming over the summer will keep it in shape. The tiny flowers are pale yellow, and are followed by fleshy red fruits if a female is grown near a male. In areas with decent rainfall, 'Fastigiata' shoots up quickly, but it also tolerates dry soils. All parts are toxic if eaten. There are several very good alternatives, some variegated.

OTHER VARIETIES *T. baccata* Fastigiata Aurea Group; *T. baccata* 'Fastigiata Aureomarginata'; *T. baccata* 'Repens Aurea'; *T. baccata* 'Summergold'.

PLANT PROFILE	
HEIGHT To 30ft (10m)	
SPREAD 20ft (6m)	
SITE Full sun to deep shade	
SOIL Fertile, free-draining	
HARDINESS Z7–8 H8–7	

T

T

Taxus baccata 'Standishii' Yew

AN EXCELLENT HEAD-HIGH, THIN, UPRIGHT YEW, 'Standishii' is a big hit with garden designers because of its slow-growing, striking shape. It can be arranged in straight, formal lines like sentries on parade, directing the eye to another part of the garden, or to provide a contrast with chunkier, rounder shapes. Its golden yellow foliage also contrasts with bluish and dark green leaves. After five years or so, 'Standishii' will probably be 12in (30cm) wide, though in time it does fatten up. For a taller, wider, faster-growing yellow, go for *T. baccata* Fastigiata Aurea Group.

OTHER VARIETY *T. baccata* 'Ivory Tower'.

PLANT PROFILE
HEIGHT 5ft (1.5m)
SPREAD 24in (60cm)
SITE Full sun to deep shade
SOIL Fertile, free-draining, tolerates alkalinity
HARDINESS Z7–8 H8–7

Taxus cuspidata Japanese yew

T

A CHUNKY, SIZEABLE YEW with dark green leaves, it makes a
powerful backdrop in large gardens. Japanese yew can be trimmed
in early and late summer to keep it reasonably shapely and to stop it
from getting out of hand. Tough and hardy, it is also an excellent
choice for those cold northern regions where *T. baccata* cannot
survive, although the Japanese yew's winter leaves may turn brown
when the temperature dives. 'Aurescens' is a 5ft- (1.5m-) high by
10ft- (3m-) wide, lower-growing alternative with a show of
yellowish shoots in early summer, which gradually end up green.

OTHER VARIETIES *T. cuspidata* var. *nana*; *T. cuspidata* 'Straight Hedge'.

PLANT PROFILE
HEIGHT 30–50ft (10–15m)
SPREAD 20–25ft (6–8m)
SITE Full sun to deep shade
SOIL Fertile, free-draining, tolerates acidity or alkalinity
HARDINESS Z4–7 H7–1

T

Thuja plicata 'Zebrina' Western red cedar

THE BRIGHT YELLOW-STRIPED LEAVES make the coniferous 'Zebrina' one of the best of the Western red cedars, but this tall, broadly conical tree must be grown in full sun or the yellow will not fully emerge. The sprays of leaves emit a scent of fresh fruit. The attractive bark is reddish brown and peels in vertical strips. The spring flowers (reddish black males and yellow-green females) are followed by brown cones. Young plants in cold areas will need some protection against cold, drying winds.

OTHER VARIETIES *T. plicata* 'Atrovirens'; *T. plicata* 'Aurea'; *T. plicata* 'Doone Valley'; *T. plicata* 'Irish Gold'; *T. plicata* 'Rogersii'; *T. plicata* 'Stoneham Gold'.

PLANT PROFILE
HEIGHT 40–50ft (12–15m)
SPREAD 12ft (4m)
SITE Full sun
SOIL Moist but free-draining
HARDINESS Z6–8 H8–6

Tilia cordata 'Greenspire' Small–leaf lime

T

A FAST-GROWING DECIDUOUS LIME, 'Greenspire' shoots up, making an architectural column of growth that contrasts nicely with fuller, spreading trees. For a taller, wider lime, go for *T. cordata*. Its growth tends to be columnar, eventually with a round crown. Both trees are covered in dark green leaves, no more than 3in (8cm) long, which turn yellow in autumn before they fall. And both have yellow midsummer flowers (loved by bees), in clusters of up to ten, followed by woody, gray-green nuts. 'Greenspire', like other lime trees, tolerates some shade, acidic soil, and is good for coppicing.

OTHER VARIETY *T. cordata* 'Winter Orange'.

PLANT PROFILE

HEIGHT 50ft (15m)

SPREAD 22ft (7m)

SITE Full sun or partial shade

SOIL Moist but free-draining

HARDINESS Z4–8 H8–1

T *Tilia* x *euchlora* Lime, Linden

AN EXCELLENT DECIDUOUS TREE, this lime is known for its
rounded shape and glossy, dark green leaves. The large-leaf lime
(*T. platyphyllos, see page 306*) attracts aphids that create a sticky dew
on the leaves that drips onto cars parked beneath, but *T.* x *euchlora*
is quite safe. And it has a midsummer attraction in its yellowish
white flowers, about ½in (1cm) across. Avoid ground that is too dry
and sites that are exposed to strong winds.

PLANT PROFILE

HEIGHT 70ft (20m)	
SPREAD 50ft (15m)	
SITE Full sun or partial shade	
SOIL Moist but free-draining	
HARDINESS Z3–7 H7–1	

Tilia henryana Lime, Linden

T

AN EXCEPTIONAL DECIDUOUS TREE, it has creamy white flowers dangling down at the end of summer and early autumn. It is also noted for its broad, rounded leaves (reddish when young) with bristlelike teeth around the edges. Although *T. henryana* can be quite a giant in its native central China, it is highly unlikely to reach more than 40ft (12m) high in the backyard and, being slow-growing, will take many years to reach even that height. Growth will be checked if it is not given shelter from cold winds.

PLANT PROFILE

HEIGHT To 80ft (25m)

SPREAD To 80ft (25m)

SITE Full sun or partial shade

SOIL Moist but free-draining

HARDINESS Z6–8 H8–6

T

Tilia oliveri Lime, Linden

ONE OF THE BEST LIMES, *T. oliveri* is deciduous, vigorous, and quickly shoots up, making a large, spreading shape. On young trees, the dark green leaves are up to 5in (12cm) long; they are even longer on mature limes, and taper to a point. They are whitish underneath, which creates a rippling effect when the leaves are being blown around. Pale yellow flowers appear in midsummer. Avoid ground that is too dry and sites exposed to strong winds.

PLANT PROFILE

HEIGHT 50ft (15m)

SPREAD 30ft (10m)

SITE Full sun or partial shade

SOIL Moist but free-draining

HARDINESS Z6–9 H9–6

Tilia 'Petiolaris' Pendulous silver lime

A THRILLING SIGHT, the pendulous silver lime soars up, making
a huge, broad column with a mass of growth and thick, weeping
branches (*see inset*). In summer it is covered by dark green leaves that
are white beneath. When the wind blows, you get a fluttering, two-
tone effect. Bees swarm down to the nectar-rich, late-summer, pale-
yellow flowers, but when they overindulge, a narcotic sets in and
they end up stumbling on the grass, dizzy and disorientated. The
towering 'Petiolaris' is only for those with huge yards.

PLANT PROFILE

HEIGHT 100ft (30m)

SPREAD 70ft (20m)

SITE Full sun or partial shade

SOIL Moist but free-draining

HARDINESS Z5–9 H9–5

T *Tilia platyphyllos* Large-leaf lime

THE BEST REASON FOR GROWING this massive, deciduous lime is that its scented, pale yellow flowers appear in midsummer, earlier than the other limes. They are followed by woody, gray-green fruits that hang on into winter. Though the common name refers to large leaves, do not expect anything dramatic, because at most they are only 6in (15cm) long. As with other limes, avoid planting on ground that is too dry and sites exposed to strong winds.

OTHER VARIETIES *T. platyphyllos* 'Aurea'; *T. platyphyllos* 'Fastigiata'; *T. platyphyllos* 'Laciniata'; *T. platyphyllos* 'Rubra'; *T. platyphyllos* 'Tortuosa'.

PLANT PROFILE

HEIGHT 100ft (30m)

SPREAD 70ft (20m)

SITE Full sun or partial shade

SOIL Moist but free-draining

HARDINESS Z2–6 H6–1

Toona sinensis Chinese toon

T

CERTAINLY NOT WELL KNOWN, this deciduous Chinese tree is actually a potential star. The leaves consist of up to 26 leaflets, which are initially bronze-red to pink, then turn glossy dark green over the summer, and end up yellow in autumn before falling. In midsummer, given a long hot spell, the small, scented, white or greenish white flowers appear in clusters up to 12in (30cm) long. *T. sinensis* prefers some shelter in windy, open gardens to keep the summer temperatures consistently up. Cigar boxes were once made from its bark.

OTHER VARIETY *T. sinensis* 'Flamingo'.

PLANT PROFILE	
HEIGHT 50ft (15m)	
SPREAD 30ft (10m)	
SITE Full sun	
SOIL Fertile, free-draining	
HARDINESS Z5–8 H12–10	

T *Tsuga canadensis* Eastern hemlock

THE EASTERN HEMLOCK GROWS BEST where it has some wind protection, and if that means a degree of shade, that's fine, because it is quite happy in these conditions. The evergreen conifer is often multistemmed, and always tall and graceful, with late-spring flowers followed by pale brown cones. Make sure the soil does not dry out. If you are considering another form of tsuga, note that some in this varied family (such as *T. canadensis* 'Cole's Prostrate') are 12in- (30cm-) high midgets. Finally, don't confuse this with the poisonous hemlock. The toxic plant—used to kill Socrates in 399 BC—is *Conium maculatum*, a biennial found in damp spots and open woods.

OTHER VARIETY *T. canadensis* 'Aurea'.

PLANT PROFILE
HEIGHT To 80ft (25m)
SPREAD To 30ft (10m)
SITE Full sun or partial shade
SOIL Rich, moist but free-draining, acidic
HARDINESS Z4–8 H8–1

Tsuga heterophylla Western hemlock

T

THOUGHT BY MANY TO BE A FINER TREE than *T. canadensis* (*see opposite*), this evergreen conifer is a quick sprinter, putting on rapid growth, but it does need some shelter to excel, and soil that does not dry out. In the right conditions, growth is huge and impressive. The leaves are glossy and dark green, and the reddish flowers are followed by ¾in- (2cm-) long, brown cones. The bark is purple-brown. It is quite happy in shade. Like *T. canadensis*, this is not poisonous, and is unrelated to the toxic hemlock.

OTHER VARIETY *T. heterophylla* 'Iron Springs'.

PLANT PROFILE
HEIGHT 70–130ft (20–40m)
SPREAD 20–30ft (6–10m)
SITE Full sun or partial shade
SOIL Rich, moist but free-draining, acidic
HARDINESS Z6–8 H8–6

U | *Ulmus glabra* 'Camperdownii' Camperdown elm

DECIDUOUS, WITH DARK GREEN LEAVES that turn yellow before
falling in autumn, the camperdown elm also has tiny red flowers in
early spring, followed by small green fruits. It is an attractive,
weeping variety that makes a relatively small and sensible choice for
an elm because if it does get Dutch elm disease (and that is very
unlikely), it will not leave a gaping hole in the yard.

PLANT PROFILE
HEIGHT 25ft (8m)
SPREAD 25ft (8m)
SITE Full sun or partial shade
SOIL Average, free-draining
HARDINESS Z4–7 H7–3

OTHER VARIETIES *U. glabra; U. glabra* 'Exoniensis'; *U. glabra*
'Lutescens'; *U. glabra* 'Pendula'.

U

Ulmus parviflora Chinese elm

UNLIKELY TO BE ATTACKED BY DUTCH ELM DISEASE, the Chinese elm has moderate growth with several attractions. The leathery, glossy, dark green leaves can be semi-evergreen, and while some may turn yellow or red in late autumn and early winter, others may hang on for longer. The bark develops flecks of orange, and sometimes a marbling of yellow-gray and cream. Tiny red flowers appear from late summer to autumn, followed by small, green, winged fruits.

OTHER VARIETIES   *U. parvifolia* 'Frosty'; *U. parvifolia* 'Geisha'; *U. parvifolia* 'Hokkaido'; *U. parvifolia* 'Yatsubusa'.

PLANT PROFILE
HEIGHT 60ft (18m)
SPREAD 25–40ft (8–12m)
SITE Full sun or partial shade
SOIL Average, free-draining
HARDINESS Z5–9 H9–5

U | *Ulmus procera* English elm

A GREAT DOMINATING BEAUTY OF A DECIDUOUS TREE, the English elm makes a dense, upright crown rich in dark green leaves, which turn yellow in the autumn before falling. Tiny red spring flowers are followed by green, winged fruits in late spring. Though it is called English, there is a good chance that it actually originates from northern Spain. Beware of planting it in areas prone to Dutch elm disease. If this illness strikes, the beetles that carry the disease should eventually die off when there are no more elms to breed in, while below-ground suckers on the affected trees may one day grow to produce replacements. Disease-resistant elms include *U. pumila* and *U.* 'Sapporo Autumn Gold'.

OTHER VARIETY *U. procera* 'Argenteovariegata'.

PLANT PROFILE
HEIGHT 40m (130ft)
SPREAD 50ft (15m)
SITE Full sun or partial shade
SOIL Free-draining
HARDINESS Z5–8 H8–1

Umbellularia californica California laurel, Headache tree

U

FROM THE WESTERN UNITED STATES, THIS EVERGREEN makes a
large, rounded shape with leathery, bright green leaves up to 4in
(10cm) long. When they are crushed, they release a sharp smell that
can give some people nausea and a headache. Its best period kicks
off in late winter, lasting into spring, when there are clusters of small
yellow-green flowers followed by purple berries. Though it is hardy,
it thrives best with some shelter in cold, windy areas where severe
frosts strike.

PLANT PROFILE	
HEIGHT 60ft (18m)	
SPREAD 40ft (12m)	
SITE Full sun	
SOIL Average, free-draining	
HARDINESS Z7–9 H9–7	

Z | *Zelkova carpinifolia* Caucasian elm

WELL SHAPED, WITH ERECT BRANCHES SHOOTING OUT of the short, sturdy trunk and making a great mass of aerial growth, the Caucasian elm has plenty of presence in summer. And in autumn, the dark green leaves, up to 4in (10cm) long, turn orange-brown before falling. The spring flowers are insignificant. Although it is called an elm, a mature tree is more likely to be toppled by a severe gale than attacked by Dutch elm disease.

PLANT PROFILE

HEIGHT 100ft (30m)

SPREAD 80ft (25m)

SITE Full sun or partial shade

SOIL Fertile, moist but free-draining

HARDINESS Z5–9 H9–5

Zelkova serrata Japanese zelkova

Z

ITS POTENTIALLY GIGANTIC, SPREADING SHAPE (*see inset*) means that the Japanese zelkova has to be grown in parkland, or on large lawns, where it makes its mark in autumn when the dark green leaves turn yellow, orange, or red. The attractive leaves are distinctive because they are edged with up to 16 teeth on both sides. The flowers and fruits are very small. Dutch elm disease is theoretically a problem, but only if you are very unlucky.

OTHER VARIETIES *Z. serrata* 'Goblin'; *Z. serrata* 'Green Vase'; *Z. serrata* 'Variegata'.

PLANT PROFILE

HEIGHT To 100ft (30m)

SPREAD 60ft (18m)

SITE Full sun or partial shade

SOIL Fertile, moist but free-draining

HARDINESS Z5–9 H9–5

The publisher would like to thank the following for their kind permission to reproduce their photographs:

(Abbreviations key: t=top, b=below, r=right, l=left, c=center, a=above, DK/RS=DK/Roger Smith Images, DK=DK Images)

3: Garden World Images (cr); **19:** DK/RS; **20:** DK/RS; **22:** DK/Andrew Butler; **27:** DK/RS; **28:** Marcus Harpur (r), Garden World Images (l); **31:** DK/RS; **34:** DK/RS(tr); **36:** Garden World Images (c), Garden World Images/Charles Hawes (tr); **43:** Photos Horticultural; **49:** DK/RS (l); **50:** DK/RS (tr); **52:** DK/RS (tr), John Glover (tl); **59:** Garden World Images; **65:** DK/Andrew Butler (c); **67:** DK/RS; **72:** Andrew Lawson (tr, c); **73:** Photos Horticultural; **77:** Eric Crichton Photos; **78:** Photos Horticultural; **80:** DK/Juliette Wade; **82:** Andrew Lawson; **88:** DK/Andrew Butler (tr); **90:** DK/Andrew Butler; **91:** DK/RS (tr); **93:** DK/Andrew Butler; **98:** Photos Horticultural; **102:** Garden World Images; **107:** DK/RS; **110:** DK/Bob Rundle; **112:** DK/RS, Jerry Harpur; **115:** DK/RS (tr); **118:** DK/Andrew Butler (tl, tr); **119:** DK/Andrew Butler; **121:** DK/Dave Watts (tl, tr); **122:** DK/RS (c), Photos Horticultural (tr); **125:** Garden World Images (tr, c); **126:** Eric Crichton Photos; **127:** DK/Andrew Butler; **129:** DK/Andrew Butler; **131:** DK/Dave Watts (tr); **133:** Photos Horticultural; **135:** Garden World Images; **136:** DK/C. Andrew Henley (tr, c); **140:** DK/RS; **141:** Andrew Lawson; **143:** DK/RS; **144:** Eric Crichton Photos; **145:** Photos Horticultural; **152:** Photos Horticultural; **153:** A-Z Botanical Collection; **155:** DK/Juliette Wade (tr), DK/RS (c) **156:** Garden World Images (c), Andrew Lawson (tr, c); **157:** Photos Horticultural; **158:** DK/Andrew Butler; **159:** DK/John Fielding; **161:** DK/Andrew Butler; **162:** DK/RS (c), Jo ʳʷ¹·· ⁻⁻ᵒrth (tr); **166:** Photos Horticultural; **168:** DK/RS ɔK/RS; **171:** DK/RS (l); **173:** DK/Andrew Butler; **180:** DK/Christine M. Douglas; **181:** DK/Andrew Butler; **182:** John Glover; **183:** Garden World Images; **185:** DK/Beth Chatto (tr, c); **187:** DK/John Fielding; **188:** DK/RS (c), John Glover (tr); **191:** Photos Horticultural; **196:** Garden World Images; **201:** DK/John Fielding; **203:** Garden World Images; **204:** DK/RS (l); **210:** DK/John Glover; **212:** DK/Andrew Butler; **215:** DK/Juliette Wade; **217:** A-Z Botanical Collection/T. Foster (l); **220:** Photos Horticultural; **225:** Photos Horticultural; **226:** DK/Juliette Wade (tr), DK/RS (c); **228:** Andrew Lawson (tr), Garden World Images (c); **231:** DK/RS (c); **240:** DK/RS; **242:** DK/Christine M. Douglas; **243:** DK/RS (tr); **245:** DK/RS; **247:** Photos Horticultural; **249:** DK/Andrew Butler (tr, c); **252:** Andrew Lawson (c), Garden World Images (tr); **254:** Photos Horticultural; **255:** DK/Andrew Butler (c); **257:** Garden World Images; **259:** DK/RS; **260:** DK/RS; **263:** Garden World Images; **264:** Photos Horticultural; **265:** Photos Horticultural (tl); **267:** DK/Beth Chatto; **268:** Garden World Images; **270:** Photos Horticultural; **271:** Photos Horticultural; **275:** DK/Andrew Butler; **276:** DK/RS (tr); **282:** Photos Horticultural; **284:** Photos Horticultural; **286:** Garden World Images; **288:** Garden World Images; **292:** DK/RS (tr), Garden World Images; **293:** DK/RS; **294:** DK/Andrew Butler (tr); **296:** DK/Juliette Wade (tr), DK/RS; **297:** DK/Juliette Wade (tr); **298:** Garden World Images; **300:** Garden World Images; **302:** Andrew Lawson, Photos Horticultural (tr); **303:** DK/Andrew Butler; **307:** DK/RS; **309:** Eric Crichton Photos; **312:** Garden World Images; **314:** DK/Andrew Butler;

All other images © DK Images.

For further information, see www.dkimages.com